108 B

STUDIES IN THE UK

Regional ec

STUDIES IN THE UK ECONOMY

Regional economics

Harvey Armstrong and Jim Taylor
University of Lancaster

Series Editor

Bryan Hurl
Head of Economics, Harrow School

HEINEMANN
EDUCATIONAL

To our parents

Heinemann Educational,
a division of Heinemann Educational Books Ltd.
Halley Court, Jordan Hill, Oxford OX2 8EJ

OXFORD LONDON EDINBURGH
MADRID ATHENS BOLOGNA
MELBOURNE SYDNEY AUCKLAND
IBADAN NAIROBI GABORONE HARARE
KINGSTON PORTSMOUTH (NH) SINGAPORE

First published 1990

British Library Cataloguing in Publication Data
Armstrong, Harvey
  Regional economics. – (Studies in the UK economy).
  1. Great Britain. Regional economic conditions
  I. Title II. Taylor, Jim, 1941– III. Series
  330.941

ISBN 0435 330063

Typeset and illustrated by Taurus Graphics, Abingdon, Oxon.
Printed and bound in Great Britain by Biddles Ltd, Guildford, Surrey

Contents

Acknowledgements

The authors would like to thank Bryan Hurl for his contribution to this booklet.

Thanks are also due to the following for permission to reproduce copyright material: *Economist* for the article on pp. 68–9; *Financial Times* for the quotations on pp. 1, 3, 19, 29; Wynne Godley for the quotation on p. 57, which appeared in *Guardian*; Halifax Building Society for the table on p. 15; Controller of Her Majesty's Stationery Office for the table on p. 53, which appeared in *British Business*, the table on p. 56, and the quotation on p. 70; *Independent* for the article on p. 29–30; *Municipal Journal* for the article on pp. 78–80; *Sunday Times* and Charles Oulton for the article on pp. 40–41 and Heath for the cartoon on p. 40; University of Oxford Delegacy of Local Examinations for the question on p. 22.

The Publishers have made every effort to trace copyright holders. However, if any material has been incorrectly acknowledged we would be pleased to correct this at the earliest opportunity.

Preface

As the 1980s progressed, the UK economy shook itself free from the shock of the 1980–81 recession and its attendant post-war record levels of unemployment. It entered a growth phase of booming output, falling inflation and rising living standards.

National growth is supposed to be good for us all – the regional multiplier shares around rising aggregate demand geographically.

And yet . . . at the same time, the regional problem which has been with us since the inter-war period stubbornly took on a new dimension. Increasingly, the 'media', when persuaded to explore north of Watford, publicized the 'north–south divide'. If prosperity rises, and spreads, then surely a divide is swamped?

Harvey Armstrong and Jim Taylor, from their perspective in Lancaster, very far north of this Severn–Humber line, analyse its causes and look critically at the abandonment of traditional post-war interventionist policy. The standard regional map of assistance is no more: a shrunken remnant with new and less generous levels of government help has replaced it and, as the UK government pulls back, so self-help or the EEC is to replace it. What will this do for regional economic disparities in the UK?

Bryan Hurl
Series Editor

Chapter One
Introduction

'Perhaps more than any other subject, the north–south divide is guaranteed to send pulses racing and temperatures rising at Westminster.

In a place where everything from the fate of donkeys to the future of football can bring MPs to boiling point, the Commons reserves a very special passion for the 'two nations' issue.
Michael Cassel, *Financial Times*, 27 January 1989

It is the purpose of this book to examine the north-south divide and the wide range of policies which have been used – or could be used – to reduce the substantial economic imbalance which exists between the northern and southern parts of Britain.

The existence of a significant regional problem in Britain has been acknowledged since the 1920s, when the decline of the old staple industries such as cotton, coal, iron, steel and shipbuilding led to the opening of a very considerable north–south divide as reflected by the relative unemployment rates in the northern and southern regions. Employment opportunities have been consistently and considerably worse in many northern parts, and this has led to successive attempts by the British government to create more jobs in areas of high unemployment. Despite these efforts, Britain is still faced with extremely severe regional problems. Indeed, the north–south divide has widened during the 1980s. Regional differences in unemployment, for example, have been far greater in the 1980s than at any time since the depression of the 1930s.

Opponents of British regional policy argue that the worsening of the divide in the 1980s is ample evidence that regional policy has been a failure – and an expensive failure at that. The assistant editor of the *Financial Times*, Samuel Brittan, wrote in March 1989:

'All too often the effect of so-called regional policies is to establish cathedrals in the desert or to enable local politicians to reward supporters with succulent contracts.'

Supporters of regional policy argue exactly the opposite. They say that

1

regional policy has not succeeded because it has been far too weak. Put simply, too little effort and too few resources have been committed to creating jobs in areas of high unemployment. It is also argued that a completely fresh approach to regional policy is now required if the trend towards the increasing concentration of jobs and people in southern parts of Britain is to be reversed. This book outlines the new approaches to regional policy which are currently being suggested by academics and by those directly involved in the economic development process.

Our first task is to examine the severity of Britain's regional problem. How deep is the divide? Is it getting any worse, and if so at what rate? Attention is initially focused upon regional differences in job opportunities since these play a crucial role in determining living standards. How substantial are the existing regional differences in job opportunities? To what extent have they changed in the 1980s? These and other issues are discussed in Chapter 2. This investigation of the north–south divide is followed, in Chapter 3, by a discussion of the case for finding a solution to regional problems based upon removing impediments to the *free operation of market forces*. After rejecting this free-market approach, Chapter 4 examines the case for *government intervention*. The various policies which have been used by successive governments to reduce regional disparities are examined in Chapter 5, which also discusses the most recent developments in policy. This is followed in Chapters 6 and 7 by a more detailed explanation of the *new forms of regional policy* which emerged in the 1980s. These brought in many new developments at the local level, as well as considerably greater involvement in regional issues by the European Community – particularly leading up to the removal of trade and other barriers within the Community after 1992. Finally, Chapter 8 suggests various ways in which regional policy could be developed in order to make it a more effective instrument for reducing regional economic disparities.

Reading list

H. Armstrong and J. Taylor, 'Regional Policy: Dead or Alive?', *Economic Review*, Nov. 1986.

N.I.E.S.R., *The UK Economy*, Heinemann Educational, 1990, Chapter 7.

Chapter Two

Regional economic disparities in the 1980s: the north–south divide

'One of the most confused notions is that of the north–south divide. It implies that virtually all the wealth is in the south, even the south-east, while the rest of the country is a zone of unrelieved devastation.

The truth is that there is an archipelago of wealth in the north, just as there is an archipelago of poverty in the south. For example, parts of Brixton or some of the council estates around King's Cross in London are as depressing as their counterparts in, say, Manchester .'
Joe Rogaly, *Financial Times*, 31 March 1987

Fact or fiction?

The above quotation correctly points out that the **north–south divide** is a gross oversimplification of reality. Pockets of prosperity do indeed exist in the north as well as pockets of depression in the south. Moreover, the fact that economic disparities are far wider *between* localities *within* regions than they are between the regions themselves suggests that we should be focusing on much smaller geographical areas than the British regions. The reason we focus on regions, however, is quite simple: it makes the discussion more manageable. Many of the key issues can be illustrated just as well by comparing the performance of regions as they can by comparing the performance of hundreds of individual localities.

In the rest of this book we shall use the official standard regions of the UK, for which statistics are readily available. There are eleven regions but, unfortunately, Northern Ireland is a very special case with special problems, so the north–south divide will refer, in the main, to the ten **standard regions** of Great Britain.

There are five regions in the 'north' – Scotland, North, Yorkshire/ Humberside, North West and Wales. There are five regions in the 'south' – East Midlands, West Midlands, East Anglia, South East and South West (see Figure 1).

Hence, even though the concept of a north–south divide is a gross oversimplification of reality, it does nevertheless focus attention on the

Figure 1 North and south, by standard region

fundamental economic imbalance between geographical areas in Britain. We should not, however, become too mesmerized by the imbalance between the two parts of Britain on each side of a line drawn from the Severn to the Humber. A thorough analysis of the 'regional problem' needs to be far more geographically sensitive than this. The concept of a north-south divide therefore refers not only to the economic gap between regions, but also to geographical variations in economic performance more generally – even within the south.

An example of the need to consider not simply *regional* disparities but disparities between localities *within* regions is provided by Table 1. This gives information about unemployment rates for counties within each region. The main point to be made is that some southern counties have unemployment rates which are as high (or higher) than unemployment rates in some northern counties. Which pockets of local distress therefore exist within the low-unemployment regions of the south?

The remainder of this chapter examines regional disparities in unemployment, employment growth, output growth and living standards. Regional disparities in these variables are intimately related, but it is worth while considering them independently since they highlight different aspects of Britain's regional problem.

Regional unemployment disparities

The divergence in economic performance between the north and the south is most clearly demonstrated by long-run trends in **regional unemployment** disparities. Figure 2 shows that regional unemployment disparities widened alarmingly during the 1980s. Past experience indicates that this is exactly what we should expect to happen since regional unemployment disparities are closely related to the national unemployment rate. As the national unemployment rate increases, regional unemployment disparities tend to widen since a national recession has more serious effects in the north than in the south. This is partly a result of the fact that northern regions rely more heavily upon industries which are highly sensitive to fluctuations in national economic activity. Manufacturing industries, for example, are more sensitive to booms and slumps than are service industries. Since northern regions depend more heavily on manufacturing industries, they are consequently more severely affected by booms and slumps.

It is no surprise, therefore, to find that the **1979–83 recession** had a far greater impact on the north. The newly-elected Thatcher government was determined to stamp out inflation and operated an extremely restrictive monetary policy (by raising interest rates to

Table 1 Percentage unemployment rates in the counties of Great Britain, 13 April 1989

SOUTH EAST		YORKS & HUMBERSIDE	
Bedfordshire	3.7	Humberside	9.9
Berkshire	2.3	North Yorkshire	5.8
Buckinghamshire	2.4	South Yorkshire	11.8
East Sussex	4.9	West Yorkshire	7.8
Essex	4.9		
Hampshire	4.2	NORTH WEST	
Hertfordshire	2.8	Cheshire	7.4
Isle of Wight	8.6	Lancashire	9.6
Kent	5.1	Greater Manchester	8.3
Oxfordshire	2.5	Merseyside	15.2
Surrey	—	NORTH	
West Sussex	2.2	Cleveland	13.8
Greater London	5.9	Cumbria	6.8
		Durham	11.5
EAST ANGLIA		Northumberland	10.9
Cambridgeshire	3.5	Tyne & Wear	12.8
Norfolk	5.6		
Suffolk	3.8	WALES	
		Clywd	9.3
SOUTH WEST		Dyfed	11.0
Avon	5.9	Gwent	10.3
Cornwall	10.1	Gwynedd	12.1
Devon	7.3	Mid-Glamorgan	12.3
Dorset	4.5	Powys	6.2
Gloucestershire	4.4	South Glamorgan	7.9
Somerset	5.2	West Glamorgan	10.7
Wiltshire	4.0		
		SCOTLAND	
WEST MIDLANDS		Borders	6.1
Hereford and Worcester	5.2	Central	11.5
Shropshire	6.5	Dumfries & Galloway	9.4
Staffordshire	6.0	Fife	11.6
Warwickshire	4.9	Grampian	5.9
West Midlands conurbation	8.9	Highland	10.5
		Lothian	8.6
EAST MIDLANDS		Strathclyde	13.4
Derbyshire	7.8	Tayside	10.1
Leicestershire	4.9	Orkney Islands	9.6
Lincolnshire	7.7	Shetland Islands	5.6
Northamptonshire	3.9	Western Islands	16.7
Nottinghamshire	8.6		

Note: Figures are not given for Surrey
Source: *Employment Gazette.*

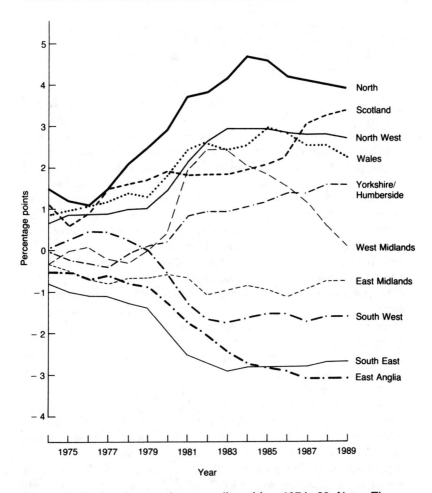

Figure 2 Regional unemployment disparities, 1974–89. Note: The vertical axis shows the regional unemployment rate minus the national (UK) rate, expressed as a percentage point difference. Source: official statistics

record levels) during the early 1980s. The effect of high interest rates was a sharp fall in both domestic demand and the demand for exports. Domestic demand fell as credit became more expensive, forcing many firms into bankruptcy; and export demand fell because of the effect of high interest rates on the exchange rate. High interest rates strengthened the demand for sterling just when oil production from the North Sea was reaching its peak, and just after the increase in world oil prices in 1979–80. The resultant high value of the petro-pound in the early

1980s had disastrous effects on Britain's exports, particularly in the manufacturing sector. Not surprisingly, the worst effects of the recession were felt in the northern regions. This is clear from the widening gap between regional unemployment rates shown in Figure 2 in the period 1979–83.

Past experience also suggests that regional unemployment disparities tend to narrow when the economy is expanding quickly, as it was during the 1986–88 recovery. The second Thatcher government abandoned strict monetary controls, with the result that national output grew rapidly (at around 4 per cent a year during 1986–88). This rapid expansion of the economy, however, has not so far been accompanied by the expected rapid reversal in regional unemployment disparities which were caused by the preceding slump. The link between regional unemployment disparities and national economic activity appears to have broken down in the mid-1980s. This is disturbing since it implies that the north–south unemployment gap could have been *permanently* widened.

The failure of the economic recovery to reduce regional unemployment disparities indicates the existence of a considerable amount of **structural unemployment** in the north. Structural unemployment occurs because of a mismatch between the demand for labour and the supply of labour. The structurally unemployed either have the wrong skills to fill vacant jobs, or they do not live in the same area as the vacant jobs. The unemployed in the northern regions suffer from both of these problems, with the result that they have been unemployed, on average, for far longer than the unemployed who live in the south.

These regional differences in the severity of long-term unemployment have important implications for regional policy since the long-term unemployed find it much more difficult to get a job than do those who have been unemployed for only a short time. This is partly because the skill gap between those in work and those out of work widens as the length of time spent out of work increases. Those with a job are able to update their skills constantly as new products and new processes are invented. The skills of those unemployed therefore become increasingly less relevant and less useful. The morale of people who are unemployed for long periods may also be damaged, and this makes the long-term unemployed less attractive to employers.

Regional disparities in employment growth

Further evidence that the economic recovery of the mid-1980s was heavily concentrated in the southern regions of Britain is provided by regional data on employment growth. Only 18 per cent of the 2.3

million extra jobs created in Britain during 1983–88 were located in the northern regions (even though these regions had 36 per cent of the civilian workforce). Employment growth in the southern regions was 13.4 per cent compared with only 4.7 per cent in the northern regions (see Table 2). Three regions in particular failed to benefit from employment growth during the 1983–88 recovery: the North West, Wales and Scotland. Virtually the same picture is obtained of the regional impact of the recovery from a whole range of economic

Table 2 Recovery from the 1979–83 recession: employment growth in UK regions 1983–88

Region	Civilian employed labour force (in thousands)		Change in civilian employed labour force (in thousands)	
	1983	*1988*	*1983–88*	*%*
SOUTH	(10322)	(11708)	(1386)	(13.4)
South East	7812	8793	981	12.6
East Anglia	782	986	204	26.1
South West	1728	1929	201	11.6
MIDLANDS	(3702)	(4177)	(475)	(12.8)
East Midlands	1583	1793	210	13.3
West Midlands	2119	2384	265	12.5
NORTH	(8707)	(9113)	(406)	(4.7)
Yorkshire/Humberside	1941	2089	148	7.6
North West	2526	2600	74	2.9
North	1148	1241	93	8.1
Wales	1014	1039	25	2.5
Scotland	2078	2144	66	3.2
Great Britain	22730	24998	2268	10.0

Note: The civilian employed labour force is the employees in employment plus the self-employed.

Sources: *Employment Gazette* and *Regional Trends*.

variables (see Table 3). Whether we look at employment growth, output growth, changes in the unemployment rate, net migration into and out of regions, or changes in the participation rate, they all point in the same direction with very few exceptions: the benefits of the recovery were enjoyed disproportionately by the southern regions.

The worsening of the north–south divide during the 1980s is confirmed by longer-term trends in employment growth. During the

Table 3 The regional impact of the 1983–88 economic recovery

Region	Change in gross domestic product (%)	Change in employment[1] (%)	Change in unemployment rate (%)	Net migration as a percentage of the working age population[2]	Change in the participation rate (1983–87)[3]
South East	22.5	10.1	-3.3	1.6	3.7
East Anglia	32.7	24.0	-3.2	3.0	7.4
South West	23.2	7.4	-2.4	5.7	0.7
East Midlands	23.2	10.2	-2.3	1.5	2.6
West Midlands	22.4	8.8	-4.4	-1.5	1.8
Yorkshire/Humberside	21.5	6.0	-1.9	-1.4	2.5
North West	16.4	0.6	-2.7	-3.0	3.7
North	14.3	5.7	-2.7	-1.9	2.0
Wales	16.6	1.8	-2.4	0.2	-1.6
Scotland	15.0	-0.1	-1.1	-2.3	-0.4
Northern Ireland	20.0	-0.4	0.9	-3.2	-2.2
United Kingdom	20.7	8.0	-2.5	0.1	1.9

Notes: (1) Includes self-employed and HM Forces. (2) Net migration figures for 1988 are based upon projection. A positive number indicates net *inward* migration; a negative number indicates net *outward* migration. (3) The participation rate is the percentage of the population of working age who are actively participating in the workforce (including the unemployed).

Sources: *Employment Gazette* (Historical Supplement 1, April 1989) for employment data; and *Regional Economic Prospects*, Cambridge Econometrics and the Northern Ireland Economic Research Centre, December 1988, for other variables.

Table 4 Changes in employees in employment (in thousands) in UK regions, 1971–88

Region	1971–79		1979–88			
	Total all industries	Change (%)	Manufacturing	Services	Total all industries	Change (%)
SOUTH	(296)	(3.2)	(−567)	(1164)	(448)	(4.6)
South East	64	0.1	−521	891	265	3.5
East Anglia	84	13.8	18	144	149	21.2
South West	148	10.4	−64	129	34	2.1
MIDLANDS	(126)	(3.5)	(−369)	(377)	(−63)	(−1.7)
East Midlands	121	8.6	−100	185	37	2.4
West Midlands	5	0.2	−269	192	−100	−4.5
NORTH	(281)	(3.0)	(−1088)	(400)	(−975)	(−10.2)
Yorkshire/Humberside	76	4.0	−251	166	−155	−7.7
North West	−6	−0.2	−349	30	−364	−13.6
North	56	4.6	−141	75	−120	−9.6
Wales	40	4.2	−96	9	−141	−13.6
Scotland	74	3.7	−208	97	−173	−8.2
Northern Ireland	41	8.7	−43	23	−22	−4.2

Sources: *Regional Trends, 1980 and 1989.*

1970s, employment growth was almost as strong in the northern regions as it was in the south (see Table 4). The picture changed dramatically during the 1980s. Between 1979 and 1988 employment levels declined in *all* northern regions, reaching an alarming rate of decline (13.6 per cent) in the North West and in Wales. The southern regions, on the other hand, experienced an increase in employment of 4.6 per cent during this period.

Further scrutiny of the changes in employment in UK regions reveals that the employment growth in the south during 1979–88 was due to a very rapid expansion of jobs in the service sector. Over a million service sector jobs were created in the south during this period, and these more than offset the loss of nearly 600 000 jobs in manufacturing. The north was not so fortunate. The loss of over a million manufacturing jobs during 1979–88 was only partially compensated by the creation of 400 000 extra jobs in the service sector. Closer inspection of the two Midlands regions indicates that employment change in the East Midlands has been more in line with the experience of the southern regions, whereas the West Midlands has behaved much more like the northern regions during 1971–88. There is some evidence, however, that the West Midlands has been regaining lost ground during 1984–89. This is very clearly indicated by the much sharper reduction in its unemployment rate than in any other region since the mid-1980s (see Figure 2).

The rapid employment growth in East Anglia during the 1980s is worth further comment, especially since this has been so remarkably out of line with all other regions. East Anglia possesses one very distinct advantage over other regions – its location. The lower costs of land, labour and premises in many parts of East Anglia compared with Greater London have induced many employers to invest in East Anglian locations rather than in the South East. East Anglia has become an overspill area for the South East. The East Midlands and the South West have also benefited from the overflow from the South East during the 1980s, though not to the same extent as East Anglia.

Regional disparities in job quality, earnings, output per head and living standards

One aspect of regional disparities which is often overlooked is that the **quality of jobs** is generally better in the south. This does not mean that low-quality jobs do not exist in the south, but simply that a greater proportion of the south's jobs are of higher quality than those in the north. This is vividly demonstrated by the regional distribution of high-skill jobs shown in Table 5. The South East is particularly well

Table 5 Percentages of total employees in Britain in various sectors, 1984

Region	High-tech manufacturing[1]	Producer services[2]	Research and development	All industries
South East	41.1	49.6	55.0	34.6
East Anglia	3.0	2.8	7.2	3.4
South West	9.3	7.0	7.7	7.4
East Midlands	5.7	4.3	4.7	7.0
West Midlands	10.8	7.6	4.3	9.4
Yorkshire/ Humberside	3.2	5.8	2.2	8.5
North West	11.8	9.2	7.0	11.0
North	3.8	3.5	3.0	5.1
Wales	3.7	2.8	1.7	4.3
Scotland	7.7	7.4	7.2	9.1
Great Britain	100	100	100	100

Notes: (1) Includes office machinery, data processing equipment, electrical and electronic engineering, aerospace equipment, instrument engineering.
(2) Includes banking, finance, insurance, business services.

Source: *Employment Gazette.*

endowed with high-quality jobs. It has 41 per cent of all high-tech jobs, 50 per cent of all jobs in producer services (such as banking, finance and commerce), and 55 per cent of all jobs in research and development – even though the South East's share of all jobs is only 35 per cent. The opposite is true of Yorkshire and Humberside and the other northern regions, which have well below their 'fair share' of high-quality jobs.

The government itself does not help matters since many of the high-quality jobs in the public sector, or supported by government funding, are themselves located in the south. A particular striking example of this is provided by the preponderance of physics-based laboratories in the southern regions. These include the Rutherford Laboratory near Oxford, the Royal Greenwich Observatory, various atomic energy and Ministry of Defence establishments such as Harwell, Culham, Winfrith, Aldermaston, Farnborough, Malvern and Porton. In addition, there is a National Physics Laboratory in Teddington, the Meteorological Office in Bracknell, the Road Research Laboratory near Watford, and several agricultural research establishments. And this concentration of government funding of science jobs in the south is reinforced by the regional bias in defence spending (though the North West also benefits from this through defence contracts won by British Aerospace).

Table 6 Regional disparities in output per head in UK regions, 1971–87

Region	GDP per head relative to the UK average		
	1971	*1979*	*1987*
SOUTH	(106.7)	(108.7)	(110.4)
South East	113.7	116.2	118.5
East Anglia	93.6	94.4	99.8
South West	94.8	91.3	94.0
East Midlands	96.6	96.6	95.1
NORTH	(93.6)	(93.1)	(90.6)
West Midlands	102.8	96.2	91.6
Yorkshire/Humberside	93.3	92.7	92.7
North West	96.2	96.1	92.8
North	86.9	90.7	88.9
Wales	88.3	85.2	82.4
Scotland	93.0	94.6	94.5
Northern Ireland	74.3	78.2	77.4
United Kingdom	100	100	100

Source: *Economic Trends*.

The fact that job quality is better on average in the south than in the north is reflected in average weekly earnings, which are 15 per cent higher in the South East than in the UK as a whole. Higher **regional earnings** are a specific feature, though, of the South East and not of other southern regions. Average weekly earnings are very much the same across all UK regions for both males and females with the exception of the South East.

Regional differences in earnings are not necessarily a good indicator of regional differences in living standards. There are two reasons for this. Firstly, earnings refer only to that section of the population which is in work. Secondly, the **cost of living** varies between regions. Taking this first point, output per head of population is a better indicator of living standards than average earnings since output per head takes dependants into account as well as workers. Table 6 clearly indicates that regional disparities in output per head are generally greater than regional differences in earnings. Output per head in the South East, for example, was 44 per cent higher than in Wales and 53 per cent higher than in Northern Ireland in 1987. Moreover, the north–south gap in output per head has been getting wider over the long term.

The **standard of living** is determined not only by earnings but also by what those earnings will buy. The price of many commodities is very much the same in one region as it is in another, mainly because transport costs are only a small proportion of total costs for the majority of products.

There is, of course, one major exception to this general rule – **house prices** vary tremendously between regions. Table 7 provides some information on regional house prices for 1989 and the percentage change during 1983–89. This regional variation in house prices means that many income earners in the south will have far higher monthly expenditure commitments than their counterparts in the north. This applies especially to those in rented accommodation and to those with large mortgage repayments. This is best reflected in the ratio of house prices to average earnings, which remained fairly stable in the northern regions during 1983–88 while increasing in the South East. Of course, those people in the south who own property will be 'better off' as a result of the more rapid increase in house prices in the south since their capital assets have appreciated faster than those of their counterparts in the north. They can realize this increase in their wealth by selling up and moving north (as many have done!).

More evidence of the north–south divide is provided by the **migration** of people into and out of regions. People of working age

Table 7 Average house prices in UK regions in the first quarter of 1989

Region	Semi-detached house (£)	All types of houses (£)	Change 1983–89 (%)
South East	85 000	89 000	159
East Anglia	72 000	76 000	183
South West	70 000	72 000	154
East Midlands	51 000	54 000	136
West Midlands	55 000	60 000	139
Yorkshire/Humberside	44 000	44 000	103
North West	41 000	45 000	79
North	39 000	38 000	63
Wales	47 000	46 000	104
Scotland	40 000	43 000	49
Northern Ireland	28 000	34 000	30
United Kingdom	51 000	60 000	118

Notes: (1) The prices of semi-detached houses are for those built after 1960 (but not new houses). (2) The percentage change in house prices is for all types of houses.

Source: Halifax Building Society, *Regional Bulletin 21*, 1989.

tend to move out of areas where jobs are scarce and into areas where they are more plentiful. It is therefore not surprising to find large numbers of young adults moving into areas such as Greater London from the relatively depressed northern regions. London exerts a strong pull on young, highly skilled and highly educated workers. This is very clearly demonstrated in Table 8, which shows that the south attracts far more than its 'fair share' of graduates compared with other parts of Britain.

Table 8 Regional distribution of graduates in Great Britain

Region	Percentage of total 1980 graduates working in region in 1986	Percentage of total GB employees, 1984	Column one divided by column two
South	50.3	42.1	1.19
East Anglia	4.8	3.4	1.41
Midlands	13.1	16.4	0.80
North	19.0	24.6	0.77
Wales	3.7	4.3	0.86
Scotland	9.1	9.1	1.00
Great Britain	100	100	1.00

Notes: (1) The data refer to graduates of UK universities, polytechnics and colleges who graduated in 1980 and who were in full-time employment in 1986.
(2) The regions are as follows: South = South East and South West; Midlands = West Midlands and East Midlands; North = Northern region, North West, and Yorkshire and Humberside. Sources: *National Survey of 1980 Graduates and Diplomats*, Department of Employment, London; *Employment Gazette*, January 1987.

Conclusion

The evidence presented in this chapter has indicated that the north–south divide is a well-established fact of life – and has been getting worse rather than better. The question we must now seek to answer is: what should the government do about the divide? Indeed, is it a true problem, and if so should the government take any action to reduce it? This we seek to discover in the next two chapters.

KEY WORDS

North–south divide	Quality of jobs
Standard regions	Regional earnings
Regional unemployment	Cost of living
1979–83 recession	Standard of living
1986–88 recovery	House prices
Structural unemployment	Migration

Reading list

The *Financial Times* regularly publishes surveys of particular localities and regions. These are an excellent source of up-to-date material on regional problems and policies.

Bazan, S. and Thirlwall, T., *Deindustrialization*, Heinemann Educational, 1989, Chapter 3.

Clark, A. and Layard, R., *UK Unemployment*, Heinemann Educational, 1989.

A. Griffiths and S. Wall, *Applied Economics* 3rd ed., Longman, 1982, Chapter 19.

Essay topics

1. What is the evidence for a north–south divide in Britain?
2. How would you attempt to measure regional disparities in living standards?
3. Did regional disparities in living conditions worsen or improve during the 1980s?
4. Discuss the causes of the widening gap between regional unemployment rates in the UK during the early 1980s. Why had these regional unemployment disparities not narrowed significantly by the end of the 1980s?
5. Why do you think the southern regions of Britain have performed better (in terms of their unemployment rates and employment growth) than the northern regions during the 1980s?

Data Response Question 1

How we live

Table 9 provides information about various economic and social aspects of each UK region. Use this table to answer the accompanying questions.

1. Examine the relationship between the unemployment rate and each of the other variables in Table 9 by plotting scatter diagrams (with the unemployment rate on the horizontal axis and each of the other variables on the vertical axis). Draw a separate diagram in each case.
2. Is the unemployment rate a useful indicator of regional disparities in economic and social welfare?
3. Is a clear north–south divide revealed by the indicators in Table 9?
4. What would you expect to happen to these economic and social indicators if the government were to be successful in reducing regional unemployment disparities?

Table 9 Economic and social indicators in UK regions (1987 or 1986–87 unless otherwise stated)

	North	Yorkshire & Humberside	East Midlands	East Anglia	South East	South West	West Midlands	North West	Wales	Scotland	Northern Ireland
GDP per head	£5389	£5615	£5762	£6047	£7182	£5698	£5549	£5622	£4991	£5725	£4690
Average weekly household income	£198	£210	£227	£221	£302	£251	225	£232	£207	£213	£208
Average weekly expenditure per person	£61.80	£63.70	£65.50	£76.20	£87.30	£75.50	£62.30	£67.70	£60.60	£64.50	£60.70
Cars per 1000 population	254	280	312	370	363	373	332	290	306	249	262
Income tax bill (average)	£1890	£1980	£1920	£2100	£2580	£2040	£1880	£1970	£1750	£1900	£1930
Burglaries per 100 000 population	2752	2143	1366	1107	1499	1269	2010	2666	1567	1929	1098
Households with dishwasher (85–86)	3%	4%	6%	8%	9%	8%	5%	5%	4%	5%	6%
Unemployed	14.0%	11.3%	9.0%	6.8%	7.1%	8.2%	11.1%	12.7%	12.5%	13.0%	17.6%
Persons covered by private health insurance	3%	6%	7%	10%	15%	8%	8%	7%	4%	4%	n/a
Age-adjusted mortality rate per 100 000 population											
Males	1268	1194	1125	1033	1055	1014	1171	1253	1179	1324	1267
Females	1224	1144	1111	1022	1041	1011	1143	1205	1123	1257	1224
School-leavers with no graded results.											
Males	12.3%	11.4%	9.5%	11.5%	10.6%	6.9%	12.0%	12.7%	19.6%	n/a	26.5%
Females	9.2%	9.4%	7.4%	7.9%	7.1%	4.9%	8.6%	9.9%	12.7%	n/a	14.2%
School-leavers intending to go on to full-time further education	23.1%	23.3%	27.9%	28.0%	31.5%	34.1%	28.4%	29.8%	31.8%	n/a	n/a

Source: *Regional Trends 24*, 1989.

Chapter Three

Reducing regional unemployment disparities: the market solution

'The time has arrived to call the regional bluff. It is individuals rather than regions who are poor, suffer or deserve help. There is no principle of human dignity that dictates equality of average living standards in geographical areas.' Samuel Brittan, *Financial Times*, 20 April 1989

The diversity of opinions

Samuel Brittan's words, set out in the quotation above, are representative of the most extreme view of those who prefer the operation of free markets to government intervention. According to these **free market-eers**, there is absolutely *no* case for government intervention to solve *regional* problems. The government should concentrate on solving the problem of poverty, and whether or not this problem has a regional dimension is irrelevant. What Samuel Brittan seems to forget, however, is that poverty is related to unemployment and that unemployment has a very distinctive geographical dimension. It tends to be very heavily concentrated in specific geographical areas. Poverty therefore has a *spatial* dimension and is consequently a genuine target for **spatially based policies**. Indeed, spatially based policies may be a very effective instrument for reducing poverty – provided they are carefully constructed.

There is considerable controversy concerning the precise form that spatially based policies should take. Those with faith in the successful operation of market forces argue that the best response to the north–south divide is to remove impediments to market forces. Any deliberate attempt by the government to reduce regional unemployment disparities *directly* will only make matters worse – according to the free marketeers. At the other extreme are the **government interventionists**, who believe that the government should take a far more active and positive approach to reducing regional disparities in living standards. Peter Walker, Secretary of State for Wales at the time of writing, is certainly in the interventionist camp. He has argued strongly for a more active regional policy:

'At the present time in Wales I am pursuing policies which are bringing a whole range of new, free enterprise activities to an area previously dominated by the nationalized industries of coal and steel. I could not do this without government intervention.' *The Guardian*, 11 April 1989

This chapter discusses the free market approach to solving regional unemployment disparities. It focuses specifically on regional unemployment disparities in order to explain how these might be expected to respond to the removal of **market imperfections**. The arguments put forward by the government interventionists are discussed in Chapter 4.

Removing market imperfections

According to elementary economic theory, regional differences in unemployment should be eliminated automatically by the interplay of market forces. This should occur in three ways. Firstly, high unemployment in the north should lead to wage reductions, the effect of which should be to increase the demand for labour. Secondly, unemployed workers can be expected to move from areas where jobs are scarce to areas where jobs are more plentiful, thus reducing the supply of labour in areas of high unemployment and increasing the supply of labour in areas of low unemployment. Thirdly, employers should move their factories from areas where wages are high to areas where wages are low. High unemployment areas should therefore experience an inflow of jobs from low unemployment areas.

According to the free marketeers, this **classical adjustment process** does not work because of the existence of impediments to the interplay of market forces. In particular, wage levels tend to be 'downwardly sticky', even in the face of very high levels of unemployment. This is partly because of national wage bargaining rather than plant-level bargaining. Wages negotiated by national unions tend to be accepted by employers in all regions, regardless of local labour market conditions. The preferred solution of the free marketeers is that policies should be introduced which make wages more flexible – downwards. Their main proposals for **wage flexibility** are as follows:

- **Unemployment benefits** (and other benefits such as housing subsidies) should be reduced in order to encourage the unemployed to take low-paid jobs and to move out of areas of high unemployment.
- **National wage bargaining** should be replaced by **local** (plant-level) **wage bargaining** so that wages can be more responsive to local labour market circumstances (i.e. wages would fall in high unemployment regions). This policy involves weakening the power of national unions by outlawing the 'closed shop', making 'secondary picketing' illegal and making ballots of union members mandatory.

- **Public sector wages** should be reduced in areas of high unemployment in order to set an example to employers in the private sector. The government would also be more inclined to transfer its own expenditure to such areas if wages were lower (particularly since labour costs form a large proportion of total expenditure in the government sector).

Problems with policies designed to make wages more responsive to market forces

Policies to make regional labour markets more competitive by removing market imperfections run into several problems. Cutting unemployment benefit, for example, would certainly provide an added incentive for the unemployed to take low-paid jobs. There is less incentive to remain unemployed when unemployment benefit is cut.

But detailed empirical research suggests that a cut in benefits would have very little impact on unemployment in high unemployment regions. There is no evidence, for example, that the high levels of unemployment during 1980–86 were a result of unemployment benefit being too high. Indeed, the ratio of unemployment benefit to average earnings was higher in the 1970s than at any time in the 1980s, even though unemployment was several times greater in the 1980s. It should also be realized that cutting unemployment benefit still further (relative to average weekly earnings) would reduce living standards for many people who are already amongst the poorest members of society. Since poverty breeds further poverty, we may reasonably question whether this would be a sensible policy.

Reducing market imperfections by encouraging local wage bargaining has more chance of successfully reducing regional unemployment disparities than one based upon reducing unemployment benefit. Regions do not have the advantage of being able to make themselves more competitive by devaluing their exchange rate (as nations do – unless they are in a rigidly fixed exchange rate system). High unemployment regions therefore need to cut their wage costs or to raise their **labour productivity** in order to compete with low unemployment regions.

The policy of cutting the wages of public sector workers in areas of high unemployment is unlikely to have much effect on regional unemployment disparities. The consequences of such a policy could in fact be harmful to high unemployment areas, since a reduction in wages would reduce the amount these workers spent within their own locality. This in turn would cause further jobs to be lost in the short run because of the **negative multiplier effect** of the reduction in spending. The multiplier process means that a loss of income from any source

21

will lead to a cut in expenditure on goods produced and services offered within the region, particularly local services. The multiplier effect may not be a large one because a considerable proportion of the expenditure of a region's residents is on goods produced in *other* regions – or indeed in other countries. Typically, we might expect a £1 cut in *initial* expenditure within the region to result in a cut of about £1.25 in *total* income in the region. But these negative multiplier effects of a cut in government expenditure within regions should not be ignored.

Data Response Question 2
Unemployment and earnings

Using the data in Table 10 below and making use of your knowledge of economics, answer the questions that follow, from the University of Oxford Delegacy of Local Examinations, Advanced Level, June 1988, Paper 3, Ref. No. 9040/3.

Table 10 Earnings, Unemployment Rates and Employment Growth in Selected Regions of the United Kingdom, 1976 and 1985.

	South East	East Anglia	East Midlands	Yorkshire/ Humberside	North	Scotland
MEN						
Gross Weekly Earnings in £						
April 1976	77.0	66.4	67.3	68.9	71.4	71.6
April 1985	213.8	182.7	175.5	180.7	179.3	189.7
Growth rates						
(% per annum)	12.0	11.9	11.2	11.3	10.8	11.4
Unemployment Rate (%)						
1976	5.5	6.1	5.8	6.8	8.8	8.5
1985	11.7	11.9	14.9	17.7	23.0	19.1
Employment						
Growth rates						
(% per annum)	0.1	0.5	−0.5	−0.6	−1.5	−0.3
WOMEN						
Gross Weekly Earnings in £						
April 1976	50.5	43.3	42.9	43.3	45.0	44.6
April 1985	140.9	118.6	114.3	117.3	119.7	119.1
Growth rates						
(% per annum)	12.2	11.8	11.5	11.7	11.5	11.5
Unemployment Rate (%)						
1976	2.3	2.8	2.9	3.4	5.2	4.8
1985	7.5	8.9	9.7	11.2	13.0	11.2
Employment						
Growth rates						
(% per annum)	1.0	1.4	1.0	0.3	0.2	1.0

Source: *Employment Gazette*

(a) (i) Compare and contrast the earnings of men and women in the various regions. [3]

  (ii) How have men's and women's relative earnings changed over the period 1976–1985? [3]

(b) How has the incidence of unemployment amongst women compared with men changed over this period? [4]

(c) (i) Would economic theory suggest that areas with lower wages should have lower unemployment? [4]

  (ii) Do the data support your answer in (c) (i)? [3]

(d) (i) Why might unemployment influence the rate of wage increases? [5]

  (ii) Do the data seem to fit the theory? [3]

The multiplier effects of the inflow of Japanese capital

One of the primary benefits of the inflow of Japanese capital into the UK is that investment levels will be higher and this will lead to the creation of more jobs. Exactly how many jobs will be created will depend upon the multiplier effects stemming from the new investment.

The way in which the multiplier operates can be demonstrated by considering the effects of the new Toyota plant to be built in Derbyshire. According to newspaper reports, 3000 jobs will be created at the new Toyota plant itself, which is to cost £700 million. Toyota will need a wide range of components and many of these will be supplied by UK producers. Most of these **intermediate inputs** will eventually come from within the UK. It is not therefore surprising that many extra jobs will be created as a result of Toyota's new plant.

The extra jobs will not, however, come only from Toyota's demand for component parts. The workers at Toyota will *themselves* be spending their wages on a wide range of goods and services, and a substantial proportion of this extra demand will remain in the UK. Indeed, a significant amount of the extra expenditure by Toyota's workforce will remain within the *local* economy. Locally-produced goods and services will be purchased by Toyota workers, many of whom will migrate into the area to be nearer their new job. The surrounding region will also benefit since the Toyota plant will draw commuters from other areas, and expenditure in nearby areas can be expected to increase. Hence, it follows that the multiplier effects of the new Toyota plant will be felt not only within the locality in which the plant is built but also in other surrounding areas. In addition, the ripples of the multiplier process will be felt in all other parts of the UK which supply component parts to the new Toyota plant in Derbyshire.

This description of the multiplier process is rather too simplistic, however, since it ignores the fact that the Toyota plant may have some negative effects on employment as well as positive effects. To the extent that an increase in the output of Toyota cars leads to a fall in the sales of other makes of car, it is likely that there will be **negative** multiplier effects in other localities. We may, for example, expect the new Toyota plant to compete with other car producers located in the UK.

The regional multiplier is similar to the standard national (income) multiplier of the textbooks. An **expenditure injection** into the East Midlands region by Toyota will have **leakages** from its income flows; these are the marginal propensities to save, tax and import (from other regions of the UK as well as abroad). The average regional multiplier for the UK regions is estimated to be 1.25.

This shows the importance of expenditure leakages from the regional economy in that they determine the multiplier magnitude of any expenditure injection (such as that in the Toyota example presented in the Data Response Question at the end of this chapter). The higher the leakages, the lower the multiplier. It is therefore highly likely that the regional multiplier will tend to be much smaller for small regional economies (which have to import a large proportion of the goods and services they need) than for large regional economies.

To return now to the argument of the free marketeers; they would suggest that *negative* multiplier effects would be small and short-lived compared with the longer-term benefits of lower wages in high unemployment regions. But this assumes that wage cuts in the public sector will automatically spread over into the private sector. Private sector employers, however, may not follow the lead set by the public sector – largely because they will foresee that wage cuts will have a detrimental effect on the morale of their workers. This fall in morale will consequently have an adverse effect on the firm's productivity. It is surely psychologically better to aim to improve competitiveness by raising productivity than by cutting wages. The new Japanese manufacturing plants which have been springing up in Scotland, Wales and the North East have certainly put paid to the notion that labour is less productive in the northern regions. Japanese multi-nationals are being increasingly attracted to the northern regions of Britain – mainly because of the availability of labour (but together with government financial assistance in many cases).

Encouraging greater labour mobility

In addition to making wages more responsive to market conditions, the free market approach supports the use of policies to encourage greater **labour mobility** – from areas of high unemployment to areas of low unemployment. If unemployed workers migrate from areas of high unemployment to areas of low unemployment, this should in theory reduce regional unemployment disparities.

It would be unwise, however, to rely upon this automatic market mechanism since past experience indicates that inter-regional migration is far too small to reduce regional unemployment differences significantly. Indeed, nearly as many people move *into* high unemployment regions as move *out* (see Table 11). This raises the question of whether the government could introduce new policies which would increase the flow of migrants from north to south. Free marketeers argue that this would have the double benefit of reducing unemployment disparities while simultaneously relieving labour shortages (and thus inflationary pressures) in areas of low unemployment.

The government could do several things to increase the flow of labour from north to south. It could provide more financial help and advisory support for the unemployed who are willing to migrate. This policy has been tried extensively over many years but has had very little success. Many migrants, for example, find it difficult to settle down in new locations and for personal or family reasons very quickly return home. Moreover, the cost of moving south for home-owners is extremely high owing to the house price differential (see Table 7 in Chapter 2). Many unemployed people in the north simply cannot afford to move to the south – accommodation costs are too high.

One way of overcoming the problems arising from the house price differential is for the government to construct more public housing, especially at the cheaper end of the housing market. Alternatively, the government could relieve the pressure in the South East housing market by allowing building in the 'greenbelt' area around Greater London. A considerable amount of land would need to be released, however, before such a policy would make a significant dent in the north–south price differential. Moreover, this would not be too popular with residents in the Home Counties who would experience a substantial loss of amenity if the **greenbelt policy** were to be abandoned. Increasing the flow of migrants from north to south in order to reduce regional unemployment disparities may therefore help to solve one problem while simultaneously creating another one.

Table 11 Migration (thousands) into and out of UK regions, 1987

Region	Inward migration	Outward migration	Balance
South West	150.9	105.2	+45.7
East Anglia	83.3	51.1	+32.2
East Midlands	105.5	86.6	+19.0
South East (excl. Greater London)	300.5	282.1	+18.4
Wales	64.2	49.7	+14.5
Yorkshire/Humberside	87.4	87.6	−0.2
West Midlands	93.2	95.0	−1.9
Northern Ireland	9.6	15.3	−5.7
North	47.7	54.0	−6.7
Scotland	47.7	62.2	−14.5
North West	82.3	110.1	−27.9
Greater London	170.1	243.2	−73.1

Note: The information in this table refers only to the movement of people between regions. Migration within regions is excluded.

Source: *Population Trends 55,* Office of Population Censuses and Surveys, Spring 1989.

A further serious objection to any attempt to reduce regional unemployment disparities by inducing an increase in north-south migration is that outward migration from areas of high unemployment would have serious detrimental effects on the economic viability of those areas. Migration tends to be selective. The people most likely to move out of high unemployment areas are the most highly skilled and most ambitious workers who already have a job. Such people move from one area to another in order to improve their career prospects. This selective nature of migration harms the long-term economic prospects of high unemployment areas, since the latter are left with a poorer quality workforce.

The geographical inertia of industry

Further evidence that the market solution to regional problems will not work is provided by the behaviour of firms. Those firms which are already established in the South East fail to respond to labour shortages in the way predicted by the free marketeers. If firms were desperately short of labour, we should expect them to transfer their operations in huge numbers to labour-abundant regions. This does not appear to happen – there is **industrial inertia**. In a recent survey of more than a hundred companies with operations in the South East, it was discovered that:

'High technology companies in the South East operating in areas of growing importance to the national economy have no desire to move out of the region. Rather, they are seeking extra space within it.' P. Cheeseright, *Financial Times*, 27 January 1989

This evidence contradicts the free market prediction that labour and land shortages in the South East will force firms to seek alternative locations and hence redress the geographical imbalance between the demand and supply for labour. It appears that firms prefer to take their chance in the very tight labour markets in the South East, expecting to attract workers from other firms or to attract migrants from other regions.

Once established in a particular location, firms are very reluctant to move to another location. This is partly because of the disruption to production and existing staff which occurs when firms transfer their operations, and partly because of inadequate information about the benefits available from moving to other regions. Smaller enterprises in particular are very reluctant to move very far; they prefer to 'struggle on'. This is exactly why regional investment incentives have been used to encourage the movement of industry from south to north. We return to this topic in Chapter 5.

Conclusion

This chapter has argued that regional disparities in employment opportunities would be less severe if regional wages responded to conditions in the labour market. Several policies have been proposed by free market economists to encourage greater wage flexibility, but there is considerable reluctance to undertake the somewhat drastic steps which have been proposed – such as substantially reducing unemployment benefit and reducing public sector wages in areas of high unemployment.

Labour and capital migration has also proved to be an insufficient mechanism for removing regional unemployment disparities. Labour should move from areas of labour abundance to areas of labour scarcity; firms should move their plant and machinery in the opposite direction. Neither of these inter-regional movements are of sufficient magnitude to put a dent in regional unemployment disparities – though the latter would undoubtedly have been worse if labour migration from north to south had not occurred.

The next chapter examines the arguments which have been proposed by those who believe that regional economic disparities cannot be left to market forces alone. Government intervention is the order of the day.

KEY WORDS

Free marketeers
Spatially based policies
Government interventionists
Market imperfections
Classical adjustment process
Wage flexibility
Unemployment benefits
National wage bargaining
Local wage bargaining

Public sector wages
Labour productivity
Negative multiplier effect
Intermediate inputs
Expenditure injection
Leakages
Labour mobility
Greenbelt policy
Industrial inertia

Reading list

Minford, P., 'State expenditure: a study in waste', *Economic Affairs*, April–June 1984.

Gibson, N., 'Administered prices and regional policy', *Economic Review*, May 1989.

Redston, C. and Thomas, D. 'Multiplier analysis at the regional level', *Economic Review*, January 1988.

Essay topics

Assume that regional unemployment disparities are partly a result of wages being too high in areas of high unemployment relative to the demand for labour in these areas.

1. What factors would help to make wages more responsive to local levels of unemployment?
2. What could the government do to help to make wages more responsive to local levels of unemployment?
3. Why might government policies to reduce the wages of public sector workers in areas of high unemployment have harmful effects on employment in these areas (at least in the short term)?
4. How would a cut in the average money wage relative to the average price level help to raise the profitability of firms?
5. Speculate on why both *real wages* and the *productivity of labour* are equally important determinants of a region's *competitiveness*.

Data Response Question 3

Japanese investment in the UK

Read the accompanying extract by Terry Dodsworth of the *Financial*

Times, and the article by Michael Harrison and Stephen Goodwin of the *Independent* (both published on 19 April 1989). Then answer the questions below.

1. Why might new jobs created by the inflow of foreign companies into Britain's depressed regions lead to job losses elsewhere in the UK?
2. Regions which are heavily dependent upon branch plants are generally regarded as being economically vulnerable. Why?
3. Fujitsu reportedly received a grant of £30 million from the UK government to induce it to locate its new plant in a British 'assisted area'. Discuss the merits of providing grants to foreign firms.

'Toyota this week, Fujitsu last. Total investment of £1 billion over a five-year period. About 4,500 jobs in employment black spots. These are figures which demonstrate beyond all doubt the scale of the new wave of Japanese investment in the UK – one that's bound to have a lasting impact on the local economy.

But they are also figures which raise a variety of reactions, not all positive. Set against the jobs they create and the new capital they provide is the fear that indigenous companies are losing their technology base or being crowded out of new markets.

Critics argue that the build-up of Japanese investment is a further step in the colonization of British manufacturing by foreign companies. And while the Government contends that ownership is irrelevant, there is widespread fear that these new UK plants will be run as remote branch divisions, far from the seat of power. British industry, it is said, may well be losing control over its own destiny.'

Toyota plant will create 6,000 jobs

Toyota of Japan, the world's third-biggest motor manufacturer, is to build a £700m car plant at Burnaston near Derby, creating at least 6,000 jobs, it was announced yesterday.

The plant, which will be producing 200,000 cars a year by the late 1990s, is the largest single investment by a Japanese company in Europe.

Lord Young of Graffham, the Secretary of State for Trade and Industry, said the project had been won "on merit". Toyota would not receive a penny of taxpayers' money, unlike Nissan, which is getting government aid to build its £600m plant in Sunderland.

It also emerged that the UK was the favourite contender for a £100m engine plant which Toyota intends to build, providing a further 200 to 300 jobs. Junji Numata, Toyota's managing director, said a site would be chosen in the next eight weeks and added: "The UK is in the lead position, I would say."

Toyota's decision to pick the 280-acre Burnaston site, on an airfield by the A38, represents a further coup for Britain, which beat off competing bids from most other countries in the European Community.

The Derby plant will begin production of a mid-sized Carina-type car in 1992. Output will rise to 100,000 a year by the end of 1995 and will double to 200,000 a year by 1997–98, with the possibility of Toyota introducing a second model. Two thirds of its production will be exported. Toyota is almost certain to opt for a single-union, no-strike deal as Nissan did at its Sunderland plant.

Lord Young said that once production reached 200,000 cars the Toyota plant would create 3,000 direct jobs and at least another 3,000 among component manufacturers. Employment in phase one will be around 1,700. Local content of the cars is scheduled to rise from 60 per cent in 1993 to 80 per cent by mid-1995, enabling Toyota to class them as European-built.

He predicted there would be no difficulties exporting the cars to the Continent, describing French opposition to imports of Japanese cars built in Britain as a "dead issue".

This follows the assurance given by France not to block shipments of

Top Japanese investments in Britain

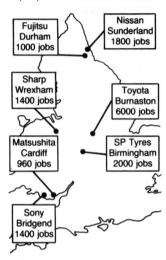

Sunderland-built Nissan Bluebirds by counting them in its stringent quota imposed on direct Japanese car imports.

The hunt by Toyota, the world's third biggest car maker, for a European production plant may have ended yesterday in the unglamorous surroundings of a disused airstrip southwest of Derby, but it in fact began as long ago as 1986.

Executives in Toyota's home city of Nagoya had witnessed the strategy being developed by their two smaller Japanese rivals – Nissan and Honda – and decided to act for fear of being frozen out of the European Community market and its 320 million consumers in 1992.

The arrival of Toyota in Burnaston will come as a particular fillip to a region not previously noted as being fashionable among foreign investors and hit by cutbacks at its biggest manufacturing companies such as

British Rail Engineering in Derby.

The announcement of the £700m Toyota plant heralds the biggest single Japanese manufacturing investment yet in Europe and confirms Britain as the number one location for inward investment from Japan.

Together with Fujitsu's decision to build a £400m microchip plant in County Durham, it will take Japanese investment in Britain comfortably above £2bn.

Chapter Four

The case for regional policy

'With the inflationary overheating of parts of England it is vital that we procure greater economic activity in those areas seeking employment.

We have two serious economic problems: inflation due to a consumer credit boom, and our worst-ever non-oil adverse balance of payments provoked again by consumer credit sucking in imports of consumer goods from overseas.

A positive regional policy helps to tackle both of these problems.'
Peter Walker, lecture to the Tory Reform Group, 10 April 1989

Rejection of the market solution

The previous chapter presented the case for tackling regional problems by removing market imperfections. Proponents of the free market approach argue that more flexible wages (downwards) and greater labour mobility are needed if regional unemployment disparities are to be reduced. The alternative approach − direct government intervention − is discussed in this chapter. As can be seen from the above quotation, it is not only opposition politicians who favour an interventionist regional policy: some members of the present government are also in favour. Not surprisingly, the interventionist approach is very popular amongst those living in areas of high unemployment. Malcolm Rifkin, Secretary of State for Scotland at the time of writing, for example, has argued that:

'At a time when costs in the South East of England are escalating, when congestion is increasing, it surely makes sense to move to Scotland. Relocation does not only make sound sense in economic terms but also helps to balance employment opportunities throughout the country and beyond that to demonstrate the political unity of the kingdom.' *Financial Times*, 27 January 1989

The remainder of this chapter is in two parts. The first part examines the *social* and *political* arguments in favour of an interventionist regional policy; and the second part examines the *economic* arguments in favour of an interventionist policy.

The social and political case for regional policy

Regional policy is now over sixty years old. It began life in 1928 when the government offered grants to unemployed miners to help them to move to areas where jobs were more readily available.

These relocation grants were followed by the establishment of Special Areas in 1934 after the depression had resulted in record levels of unemployment. Areas which were heavily dependent upon the old staple export industries – such as textiles, shipbuilding, coal, iron and steel – experienced incredibly high unemployment rates. Policies were therefore introduced in order to stimulate the growth of new industries in these areas. Keynes wrote in 1937: 'To remedy the condition of the distressed areas, *ad hoc* measures are necessary.'

The prime motive behind the pre-Second World War approaches to regional policy was the improvement of employment prospects for people located in areas of high unemployment. The same motive has been at the heart of regional policy throughout the post-war years and remains the primary justification for a regional policy based upon direct government intervention right up to the present day.

A variety of arguments have been used to justify creating jobs in areas of high unemployment. Firstly, an **interventionist policy** can be justified on **equity** grounds. Persistent regional disparities in unemployment have generally been regarded as being in some sense unfair, and there has consequently been a desire to see a fairer distribution of income and employment opportunities between the British regions. As might be expected, the sense of injustice has been felt mainly by those living in the high unemployment regions.

Secondly, regional policy has been promoted on social grounds since it is widely believed that unemployment contributes to **social problems**. The positive correlation between social problems and unemployment means, for example, that the highest crime rates and poorest health are likely to occur in the areas of highest unemployment. These social problems are made worse by the geographical concentration of unemployment, especially in the inner areas of the major conurbations. Unemployment and poverty reduce motivation and destroy ambition. Once it gathers momentum, the downward spiral of economic decline becomes increasingly difficult to reverse.

Thirdly, the case for an interventionist regional policy can be made on the grounds that political stability and national unity requires regional disparities in living standards and job opportunities to be kept within reasonable limits. If these limits are breached, large sections of the population become alienated and begin to demand their political independence since they believe they are able to manage their own affairs more capably than the national government.

These social and political arguments in favour of an interventionist regional policy should not be underestimated. The persistence of regional unemployment disparities over many decades is generally regarded as undesirable since they result in more severe social problems in the north than in the south. In addition, they sow the seeds of political disunity and are an excellent weapon for independence movements (in Scotland, Wales and Northern Ireland).

The economic case for regional policy

There are three main economic arguments in favour of an interventionist policy.

Regional policy could help to raise national output

The first and most obvious economic argument is that high levels of unemployment, wherever they exist, represent a waste of the nation's resources. A reduction in unemployment through the creation of more jobs would result in more output being produced. **National output** would be higher and everybody would be better off. Even those already in employment would be better off, since the fall in unemployment benefit paid out by the government would make lower demands on the taxpayer.

A general idea of the benefits to be obtained by reducing the unemployment rate to the national average in regions of high unemployment is provided in Table 12. If the unemployment rate were to be reduced to 8 per cent, for example, in all those regions with an unemployment rate above the national rate, unemployment in this group of regions would fall from 1 471 000 to 1 115 000 – a reduction of 356 000. If the unemployment rate were to be reduced to 7 per cent in all these regions, unemployment would be 976 000 – a reduction of 495 000. This would indeed be a substantial gain to the economy.

In addition, a reduction in the unemployment rate tends to be accompanied by an increase in the **participation rate** (i.e. the proportion of people of working age who are in the labour force). As more jobs become available, people who had not previously been in the *recorded* labour force decide to seek work. For every two unemployed people who get jobs, another person tends to be pulled into the workforce. This implies that a reduction of unemployment in high unemployment regions would have an even greater effect on employment than is indicated by the *actual* reduction in unemployment. The gains to the economy in terms of extra output being produced would therefore be greater than indicated by the reduction in unemployment.

Table 12 The effect on unemployment of reducing the unemployment rate in regions of high unemployment

Region	Unemployment rate 1988 (%)	Number unemployed (thousands) 1988	Reduction in the number unemployed (thousands) if the region's unemployment rate was reduced to:	
			8%	7%
West Midlands	8.5	230	14	41
Yorks/Humberside	9.5	226	36	59
North West	10.7	322	81	111
North	11.9	174	57	72
Scotland	11.2	280	80	105
Wales	10.5	126	30	42
Northern Ireland	16.4	113	58	65
Totals		1471	356	495

Source: Unemployment data obtained from *Employment Gazette* (Historical Supplement 1, April 1989).

Regional policy could help to reduce inflationary pressures

The second major economic argument in support of an interventionist regional policy is that a more even geographical distribution of the demand for labour would reduce **inflationary pressures**, thereby allowing the economy to grow at a faster rate. One of the primary costs of inflation is that the government has to deliberately restrict economic activity in order to bring inflation under control. This is the familiar stop-go policy of the 1960s and 1970s. Output growth was much steadier in the UK during the 1980s (from 1983), but the consequence of rapid output growth during the period 1987–89 was a revival of inflationary pressures as the economy's ability to produce output was pushed towards its limit. The reduction in income tax rates in the 1987 and 1988 Budgets, coupled with a lax monetary policy in the wake of the 1987 Stock Market crash, led to an expansion in output which the economy could not sustain.

The shortage of **productive capacity** in the British economy in 1989 is vividly reflected by the Confederation of British Industry's index of **capacity utilization**. (See Figure 3 – The CBI index is the percentage of respondents who said that they were not working below 'a satisfactory full rate of operation'. The responses are weighted by the employment level in each industrial sector.) This shows that the capacity utilization rate in the manufacturing sector was higher during 1988 and 1989 than at any time since the peak of the 1973 boom – widely regarded as contributing considerably to the very high inflation rates recorded in the mid-1970s. In other words, output growth outstripped the growth in the underlying capacity of the economy to produce output. This has also been reflected by the rapid decline in unemployment since 1986.

The downside of this fall in unemployment, however, has been an increase in wage pressures in areas of labour shortage, especially in the labour-scarce South East. With unemployment rates below 3 per cent in several counties (Berkshire, Buckinghamshire, Oxfordshire and West Sussex), and even below 2 per cent in several travel-to-work areas (e.g. Aylesbury, Crawley, Tunbridge Wells and Winchester), it is crystal-clear that the rapid output growth experienced in 1987–89 ran into serious inflationary problems. Output growth had to be cut back.

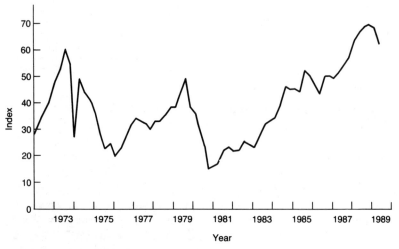

Figure 3 The CBI index of capacity utilization

The very high levels of demand in the South East are also reflected in the far faster growth in **house prices** in that region (and in adjacent regions) than in northern regions. House price inflation has also been high in the West Midlands and in Wales, even though unemployment rates were very high in those two regions during the 1980s (see Table 7 in Chapter 2). Unemployment has been falling rapidly in the West Midlands, however, since 1986, and Wales has experienced a substantial net inflow of migrants (see Table 11 in Chapter 3), many of whom are retired persons.

But does output growth have to be cut back in *all* regions? There is still plenty of unused labour available in the north which could be used to raise national output. Indeed, this is one reason why Japanese manufacturing firms have recently been seeking locations for their new plant in areas of relatively high unemployment such as South Wales, Derbyshire and Durham. Although it is highly unlikely that national output growth can be sustained at levels achieved since 1986 (i.e. over 4 per cent), there is still a substantial amount of unused labour available in areas of high unemployment which could make a significant contribution to raising national output. But it will only be possible to achieve this through policies that are spatially discriminating. A cut in demand in the economy as a whole could be accompanied by a policy of stimulating employment growth *in areas of high unemployment.*

One possibility is to move the demand for labour away from the South East – and who better to set an example than the government itself:

> 'The decision announced this month by Mr John Moore, Social Security Secretary, to move more than 1000 social security jobs out of London reflects the major problems faced by employers competing for staff in the South East.' Andrew Taylor, *Financial Times*, 27 January 1989

Moving 1000 civil service jobs out of London would, however, make only a slight impact in the excess demand for labour. A more comprehensive strategy for shifting civil service operations from south to north is required if it is to have a significant and lasting effect on reducing pressure in southern labour markets.

Regional policy could help to optimize the use of social overhead capital

Regional policies have been justified on the grounds that they help to discourage potentially costly migration. Additional investment is needed for every additional person who moves into the south since **social overhead capital** (schools, hospitals, houses, recreational facilities, etc.) is already heavily utilized in the south, particularly in the South East.

One of the most convincing indicators of the pressure on social overhead capital in the south is the high degree of **travel congestion** – on the roads, on the railways and at the airports – especially at peak travel times. Indeed, some of these transport facilities are extremely *over*-utilized at peak travel times. In addition, the rapid growth of southern England in the 1980s has put immense pressure on the London 'greenbelt' because of the incredibly high price of land in the Greater London area. Excessive growth in the South East has resulted, therefore, in serious **negative externalties**, which arise when the actions of some individuals impose costs on others, as in the cases of congestion and pollution.

Stimulating the economic revival of the north would help to relieve this pressure on the South East, thus helping to solve two problems at the same time. One rather obvious example of how this could be done is to allow more international air traffic to fly into and out of Manchester International Airport and to operate much stricter controls on further expansion at Heathrow and Gatwick. It seems crazy for northerners and midlanders to have to use the already overcrowded facilities of the Greater London transport network when Manchester airport could do the job far more effectively.

Some economists have argued that the problem of labour shortages (and hence inflationary pressures) in the South East could be most easily relieved by simply making more land available for house-building. This would reduce the pressure on house prices at one stroke and so remove a major deterrent to north–south migration. Labour shortages would thereby be relieved in the south while reducing labour abundance in the north.

Land from the Greater London 'greenbelt' could be made available quickly. This is not the case, however, with the provision of social overhead capital, which could not be increased quickly enough to cope with the extra flow of migrants from the north. Moreover, relieving the pressure on social overhead capital would not cure the underlying problem. Congestion is just the symptom of over-rapid growth in the South East; and this will continue unless the underlying problem (unbalanced regional growth) is tackled head-on.

Conclusion

The existence of serious and persistent regional economic imbalances presents the policy-maker with a choice between:

- leaving regional problems to be solved by free market forces; or
- attempting to make the north economically stronger and more capable of competing on equal terms with the south.

Chapter 3 argued that leaving regional problems to free market forces might make matters even worse – especially if the government continuously responds to the pressure on resources in the South East by offering temporary relief (such as widening the M25 motorway and allowing parts of the London 'greenbelt' to be used for new housing).

The present chapter has argued that a strong economic case can be made in support of a well-considered regional policy. An efficient and effective regional policy should in principle lead to a more optimal use of the nation's resources. In particular, unemployment should be lower in aggregate and social overhead capital should be better used.

But whether these aims are achieved depends upon whether such an efficient and effective regional policy can be devised. The next chapter discusses and evaluates current regional policy in the UK.

KEY WORDS

Interventionist policy	Productive capacity
Equity	Capacity utilization
Social problems	House prices
National output	Social overhead capital
Participation rate	Negative externalities
Inflationary pressures	Travel congestion

Reading list

Foley, P., 'Two nations?', *Lloyds Bank Economic Bulletin*, 1987.
Clark, A. and Layard, R., *UK Unemployment*, Heinemann Educational, 1989, Chapter 2.

Essay topics

1. What arguments would you use in support of having a regional policy in Britain?
2. How might a policy aimed at reducing the demand for labour in the south, while simultaneously increasing the demand for labour in the north, help to relieve inflationary pressures?
3. Why might a policy of creating jobs in the north be more beneficial to the nation as a whole than encouraging unemployed persons in the north to move south (e.g. by making more land available for house-building in the south)?

Data Response Question 4

House prices and full employment

A superficial reading of the newspaper article below from *The Sunday Times*, of 12 November 1989 seems to offer contradictions, for example:

1. How can full employment co-exist with 'entering a recession'?
2. Normally it is high house prices in the south that are a barrier to unemployed northerners moving south for jobs. Where, on the cartoon, are the points of the compass?

3. If southerners move north will this make the 'north–south' divide worse or better?
4. The article wants you to believe that 'The List' of full employment towns contradicts the 'north-south' divide. On a blank map of Britain mark this divide. Mark on the 66 towns. What is your conclusion?

Full employment bridges housing gap

If we are supposed to be entering a recession, 66 towns in Britain have not yet got the message. Instead of closures and lay-offs, these towns are celebrating their defeat of the dole queue.

Two years ago, when economic confidence was high, virtually no region had full employment. Today, however, despite forecasts of a gloomy future, many areas are booming. And not just in the south of England.

As John Major continues Nigel Lawson's tight economic regime, figures released by the Department of Employment show that from Penrith in Cumbria to Harrogate in North Yorkshire, Spalding in Lincolnshire, Chelmsford in Essex, Tunbridge Wells in Kent and Honiton in Devon, everyone has a job.

There are also indications that the number of full-employment towns will continue to grow. Five months ago, there were only 22 British towns – most of them in the southeast – with less than 3% unemployed, the recognised official full employment level.

The northern towns with full employment, most of them in North Yorkshire, have also created another trend. Two years ago, southerners could buy a home in the north on a whim. The difference in house prices between north and south meant that anyone making the move could pocket a huge profit on their housing deal.

Today, that pattern has been overturned, with northern homes, still rising in value, rarely being bought by southerners because of the depressed state of the housing market in the south.

It has long been the case that boom towns such as Crawley in Sussex have suffered from labour shortages because of a lack of housing and high house prices. With rising mortgage rates causing stagnation in the housing market, southerners tempted by job availability and the improved quality of life in the northern full-employment towns find they cannot move there either.

Rob Humphries, a 31-year-old electronics engineer, is one such Yorkshire migrant who has suffered because of the depressed housing market in the south. Attracted by the way of life in Yorkshire and the knowledge that he could get a job, he moved last February to Kirkbymoorside, a small town between two of the full-employment towns, Helmsley and Pickering, on the north Yorkshire moors.

It has not been a successful move.

While his three-bedroomed home in Aldershot, Hampshire, remains unsold, with the value down £7,000 to £70,000, Humphries is living in a bed-sit. Paying £10 a night, with no cooking facilities or a telephone, he is praying that someone will buy his home. "I am watching the value of my place in Aldershot fall, while the houses I might have bought up here get more and more expensive. You can't help wondering if it's all worthwhile."

While Humphries decided to risk taking a job with Slingsby Engineering in Kirkbymoorside, other southerners have put off moving to the full-employment towns in Yorkshire because they cannot find a house there.

Some companies are reluctant to set up in an area with such a limited labour market. Although there is still a large pool of unskilled labour in North Yorkshire, skilled workers are more difficult to find, with companies having to recruit from farther afield.

Peter Evans, research director at Debenham Tewson & Chinnocks, the international property adviser, said: "There is serious concern that much of the development activity and many of the plans to develop new business parks are being sited in areas of full employment. There may be a significant mismatch and the labour market will be unable to supply the people to work in this new commercial space."

THE LIST

The department of Employment's list of towns with full employment:

Andover, Aylesbury and Wycombe, Banbury, Basingstoke and Alton, Bedford, Bicester, Blandford, Bury St Edmunds, Cambridge, Chard, Chelmsford and Braintree, Cheltenham, Chichester, Chippenham, Cirencester, Clitheroe, Crawley.

Devizes, Diss, Evesham, Guildford and Aldershot, Harrogate, Haverhill, Heathrow, Hertford and Harlow, Hitchin and Letchworth, Honiton and Axminster, Huntingdon and St Neots, Ipswich, Kendal, Kettering and Market Harborough, Leek, Malton, Milton Keynes.

Newbury, Newmarket, Northallerton, Northampton, Oxford, Penrith, Pickering and Helmsley, Poole, Reading, Ripon, Salisbury, Settle, Shaftesbury, Skipton, Slough, South Molton, Spalding and Holbeach, Sudbury, Swindon.

Tunbridge Wells, Uttoxeter and Ashbourne, Wareham and Swanage, Warwick, Watford and Luton, Wellingborough and Rushden, Winchester and Eastleigh, Windermere, Woodbridge and Leiston, Worthing, Yeovil, Brecon, Newtown.

© Times Newspapers Ltd. 1989.

Chapter Five
The development of regional policy in the 1980s

'*Regional policy has become more selective with more attention being paid to cost effectiveness.*' Treasury *Economic Progress Report,* August 1989

The historical background
Fundamental changes were made to British regional policy during the 1980s. Traditional policies of the type that had existed since the late 1920s were radically altered.

The origins of traditional regional policy lie in the Great Depression of the late 1920s and early 1930s. In 1928, the government made grants available to unemployed miners who were willing to migrate to other regions in order to find work. When this policy proved a failure it was gradually replaced by policies designed to generate jobs in the high unemployment areas. So-called **Special Areas** were set up in 1934. This policy of 'taking work to the workers' was greatly strengthened at the end of the Second World War, and it continued in existence – sometimes strong, sometimes weak – from 1945 until 1983. Four main phases in post-war regional policy can be identified.

Phase I: 1945–51
This was a period of very active regional policy, with Labour governments grappling with severe problems as a result of post-war demobilization and reconstruction.

Phase II: 1952–59
There followed a period of weak regional policy. The economy was growing steadily, unemployment was low in all regions, and many began to think that regional problems had been solved.

Phase III: 1960–76
This was the hey-day of British regional policy. Successive govern-ments of all political persuasions made powerful and sustained

attempts to eliminate regional disparities.

Phase IV: 1977–83
The fourth phase was characterized by disillusionment with traditional regional policy. High national unemployment and a dearth of new manufacturing investment projects conspired to weaken regional policy.

Features of traditional regional policy
In order to gauge the degree of success of traditional regional policy, it is important to understand what it was attempting to achieve and the weapons it had at its disposal.

As has been shown in Chapter 4, regional policies can have several objectives, but the principal one is **job creation** in areas of high unemployment. Unlike many other European Community countries where the main problem has been job losses in the agricultural sector, Britain's unemployment problem has resulted from the decline of *manufacturing* industries. Traditional regional policy was therefore designed to provide jobs for workers with industrial skills who were used to working in a factory environment. Traditional regional policy thus had the following distinctive features:

1. An emphasis on **inward investment**
Firms from prosperous parts of Britain and from overseas were seen as the main sources of new jobs for the old industrial areas.

2. An emphasis on manufacturing
Since the unemployed were mainly blue-collar workers and had industrial experience, the new firms were to be manufacturing activities, although not in the old staple industries such as steel and shipbuilding.

3. An emphasis on industrial **location controls** *and on* **investment subsidies**
The policy was a combination of the carrot and the stick. On the one hand, strict controls were imposed on the location of industry in the South East and West Midlands: manufacturing firms had to apply for Industrial Development Certificates if their plans for new buildings in these areas exceeded a certain size. On the other hand, manufacturing firms were also offered substantial inducements to locate their new plant in designated **Assisted Areas**. The main inducement was in the form of a subsidy on all new investment in manufacturing. Employment subsidies were also available at certain times, the main one being the Regional Employment Premium in the period 1967–76.

4. An emphasis on automatic rather than selective assistance
The main incentives were automatic in nature. Civil servants were only rarely allowed to pick and choose which firms to help. The most famous automatic subsidy was the Regional Development Grant (1972–88).

5. Strong central government control
Local authorities were given almost no role to play (except the physical provision of serviced sites for factories). Until the mid-1970s, regional development agencies were almost non-existent.

6. Assisted areas defined very broadly
Help was not ruthlessly targeted on 'blackspots'. For example, in 1979 the assisted areas contained 47 per cent of the British working population.

7. Service sector firms, small firms and technical innovation all neglected
Depressed areas, it was thought, could not be expected to regenerate spontaneously 'from within'. Little help was therefore targeted on existing local firms or on new small firms.

An assessment of traditional policy
During the 1960s and 70s, traditional regional policy was regarded as being generally well thought out and reasonably successful in achieving its major objective of creating jobs in areas of high unemployment.

The sudden increase in regional unemployment disparities during the 1979–81 slump, however, led directly to the claim that traditional policy had been a failure, whereas a possible counter-argument would be that regional unemployment disparities could have been even wider if regional policy had not been in operation. Is either argument correct?

The creation of jobs
Some attempts to assess the effectiveness of regional policy have centred on trying to estimate what *would have happened in the absence of regional policy.*

Using this 'counterfactual' approach, Cambridge University economists estimated that hundreds of thousands of jobs *were* created in the Assisted Areas as a direct result of investment subsidies, labour subsidies and controls on the location of industry. They calculated, for example, that these policy instruments led to the creation of 784 000 jobs in the Assisted Areas during 1960–81. Though some of these jobs disappeared with the subsequent contraction of firms, over 600 000 were estimated to be still in existence in 1981.

Just how many of these additional jobs were entirely new and how many were jobs which would otherwise have been created in other regions (i.e. in non-assisted areas) is unknown; but it seems likely that a large proportion of 'new' jobs created in Assisted Areas were *diverted* rather than *created*.

Movement of industry into the Assisted Areas

Since one of the primary aims of regional policy has been to encourage more manufacturing industry to move to Assisted Areas, it is useful to examine actual industrial movement over the long run.

Figure 4 shows both the total number of manufacturing establishments moving between the UK regions and the movement into designated Assisted Areas. The overall long-term trend is clearly correlated with the various regional policy phases: the dip in the 1950s reflects slackening of regional policy after the immediate post-war

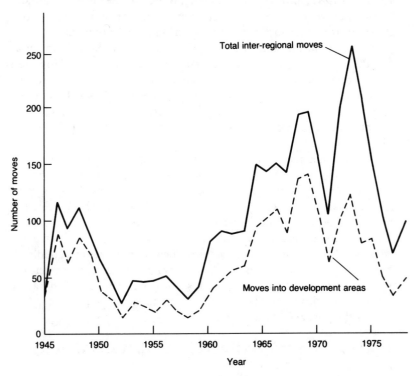

Figure 4 Inter-regional movement of manufacturing establishments in the UK, 1945–78. Source: *The Effects of Government Regional Economic Policy* by B. Moore *et al.*, HMSO, 1986

attempts to induce firms to move; and the substantial increase in industrial movement during the 1960s followed by the sharp fall in the 1970s is consistent with the rise and fall of traditional regional policy during these two decades.

Research into the effectiveness of specific regional policy instruments indicates that controls on the location of industry and investment grants have been the two most important policies in creating new jobs in Assisted Areas during the post-war era. These instruments have helped to renew the industrial base of the areas assisted, and there can be little doubt that these areas would have been in a far worse state at the present time if there had not been a regional policy in operation.

The cost per job created

According to the 1983 White Paper, *Regional Industrial Development* (Comnd 9111), over £20 billion was spent on regional policy between 1960 and 1981; and since 1981, expenditure has averaged about £0.5 billion per year. Have taxpayers got value for money from this expenditure? What sort of return has the taxpayer obtained?

Estimates indicate that the **cost per job** may have been as much as £40 000 (at 1988 prices), which at first sight seems very high. However, the cost-per-job calculations are based on the *gross* costs to the Treasury (i.e. to the taxpayer), whereas it is *net* costs which are more appropriate. Each extra job created by regional policy means higher tax revenue and lower expenditure on unemployment and related benefits. These 'clawbacks' need to be subtracted from the gross exchequer costs if the *true* financial cost to the Treasury is to be calculated.

Moreover, before an accurate assessment can be made of the net benefits flowing from regional policy, we need to know how long the new jobs last and to what extent the extra jobs created have helped to protect other jobs in the Assisted Areas. It is likely, for example, that investment subsidies in some cases have led to fewer workers being employed because of the introduction of new labour-saving technology. Yet without the new technology, firms may have gone out of existence – with a consequent much larger loss of jobs. The problem facing researchers is how to obtain accurate estimates of the jobs 'saved' as well as the jobs actually created.

Towards a new regional policy: the 1984 and 1988 reforms

Traditional regional policy came under increasing attack in the late 1970s and early 1980s – especially after the return of Mrs Thatcher's first government in 1979. From 1979, three major sets of reforms were introduced, first in 1979 by Sir Keith Joseph and then in 1984 and 1988 under Mr Tebbit and Lord Young respectively.

The 1979 reforms were much less radical than those of the 1980s. They were almost wholly a package of cuts – cuts in total expenditure on regional policy, cuts in the extent of the Assisted Areas, cuts in the investment grant rates, and a relaxation of controls on the location of industry.

Table 13 Summary of the 1984 reforms

Regional Development Grant (RDG)	• Certain service industries made eligible for RDGs alongside manufacturing industries (e.g. banking, finance, insurance, business services, industrial research and development).
	• Maximum grant reduced from 22 to 15 per cent.
	• Cost-per-job limit of £10 000 imposed on RDGs. Firms with under 200 workers exempt from this limit on projects up to £0.5 million.
	• A grant of £3000 for each new job created available in Development Areas as an alternative to the RDG. Firms receive whichever grant is the most favourable to them.
	• Replacement or modernization projects not eligible for assistance unless they lead to job creation.
Regional Selective Assistance (RSA)	• Expenditure on RSA to be increased relative to expenditure on RDGs. Switch in emphasis from automatic to selective grants, designed to make regional policy expenditure more cost-effective.
	• RSA to be used to protect existing jobs as well as creating new jobs.
Policy towards small firms and innovation	• New methods of encouraging the growth of small firms and the creation of new firms in Assisted Areas to be explored.
	• Similar schemes for encouraging technological innovation also to be examined.
Designation of Assisted Areas	• Substantial changes to delineation of Assisted Areas.
	• Special Development Areas abolished and many Development Areas converted into Intermediate Areas (not eligible for RDGs).
	• Parts of West Midlands designated as Intermediate Area for first time.
Expenditure on regional policy by Department of Trade & Industry	• Substantial reduction in regional policy expenditure planned for 1985/86–1987/88. Cuts of up to £300 million (from almost £700 million in 1983/84).

Source: Department of Trade and Industry, *Press Notice 681*, 28 November 1984.

Table 14 Summary of the 1988 reforms

- Regional Development Grant abolished. Savings in expenditure to be transferred (at least initially) to other regional assistance schemes.
- Small firms under 25 employees:
  (a) eligible for 15 per cent investment grant up to a maximum of £15000;
  (b) eligible for an innovation grant of 50 per cent up to a maximum of £25000 to support new products and new methods of production.
- Firms with under 500 employees will qualify for grants to meet the cost of employing management consultants under the Business Development Initiative Scheme: two-thirds of the cost to be met by the government (compared with one-half in non-assisted areas).
- Regional Selective Assistance: more money to be made available to offset the reduced expenditure on Regional Development Grants. Only projects that would not otherwise go ahead to be supported.

Source: *DTI – The Department for Enterprise* (Cmnd 278), HMSO, 1988.

Taken together, the 1984 and 1988 reforms represent the most radical changes to British regional policy in its sixty-year history (see Tables 13 and 14). The new regional policy which began to emerge as a result of the 1984 and 1988 reforms had the following characteristics.

Reduced spending on regional policy

This is clearly revealed by Figure 5. Even the increases in spending in Britain by the European Community's Regional Fund and by the regional development agencies in Scotland and Wales were not sufficient to offset the decline in government spending.

The government has defended its cuts in various ways. Firstly, it has been argued that investment subsidies (notably the Regional Development Grant) were not cost-effective. Anecdotal evidence of wasted subsidies – such as the large grants paid to oil companies in Shetland and around Aberdeen – is often quoted. Secondly, the economic logic of subsidizing *capital* investment in areas of high unemployment has been questioned. Job losses can arise as firms use the subsidies to switch from labour-intensive to capital-intensive production methods.

This argument, however, is based entirely on the *substitution effect* of a subsidy: as the prices of capital goods fall relative to wages, firms have an incentive to switch from labour to capital inputs. This over-simplifies reality, since capital subsidies have one primary advantage over labour subsidies – they raise a region's competitiveness by stimulating the use and development of new technology. In addition, capital subsidies may lead to significant *indirect* effects on job creation through input-output linkages between firms. The growth of capital-intensive firms may lead to more inputs being purchased

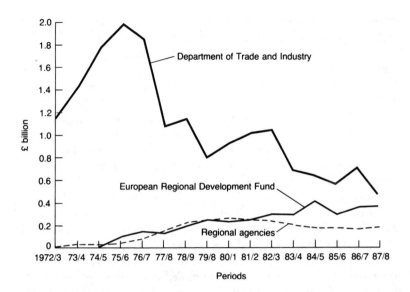

Figure 5 Regional policy expenditure in Britain at constant 1988 prices, 1972/73 to 1987/88. Source: *Regional Policy and the North–South Divide* by H. Armstrong and J. Taylor, Employment Institute, 1988

Notes: Department of Trade and Industry expenditure refers to payments actually made under the main DTI schemes (e.g. Regional Development Grants and Regional Selective Assistance). European Regional Development Fund expenditure refers to allocations made. Actual payments lag behind these allocations. Regional agencies expenditure refers to grants made to the Scottish and Welsh Development Agencies by the UK government. These grants understate the total spending by these two agencies.

from labour-intensive firms, such as commercial and other local services.

Restriction of the areas eligible for regional assistance

Figure 6 shows the Assisted Areas before and after the 1984 reforms. An increase in eligible areas in the West Midlands in 1984 was more than offset by substantial cutbacks elsewhere.

Abolition of automatic investment grants and location controls

These two great standbys of traditional regional policy were abolished. All grants were to be *discretionary*. Civil servants decided which firms could receive assistance, and on what terms, through the Regional Selective Assistance Scheme.

Switch of emphasis towards the service sector, small and medium-sized enterprises, and technical innovation

A far wider range of service sector firms were now eligible for assistance and stood on equal terms with firms in the manufacturing sector – a welcomed change to regional policy. Between 1971 and 1987, employment in service industries increased by 30 per cent while employment in manufacturing fell by 38 per cent. Alongside this switch to targeting growing sectors, emphasis swung away from inward investment and towards *indigenous* development. Depressed areas were now expected to find their own salvation, and this was to be accomplished in three ways.

Firstly, a key role was given to small firms, particularly to entrepreneurs setting up their own new small firms from scratch. Secondly, an **enterprise culture** was to be fostered in the depressed areas, the new small and medium-sized enterprises (SMEs) being the key to this. In addition, initiatives such as Enterprise Zones and Freeports – zones of lower taxes, simplified government planning and an absence of other bureaucratic controls – were experimented with extensively in the 1980s. Thirdly, existing firms were to be encouraged to adopt the very latest **technical innovations**. The 1988 reforms, in particular, were directed towards encouraging the growth of small firms and stimulating innovation.

These new policies were (and are) in part an ideological statement by the government in power. They also reflect a fear that traditional regional policy, with its restrictions on investment in the south and its subsidies designed to lure firms northwards, may in the past have damaged industry in the more prosperous areas. Traditional regional policy was also often accused of creating a branch plant economy in the north – plants which would rapidly be shut down at the first hint of a recession. Ironically, the new emphasis on indigenous development has coincided with a wave of Japanese and United States inward investment in branch plants designed to serve the European Community market.

Other changes

The European Community, local authorities and regional agencies have been allowed to expand their activities in the depressed areas as British government support has been cut. Regional policy in Britain is now in the hands of several different types of government authority.

A critical look at the small firms policy

In the new regional policy now emerging, small and medium-sized enterprises (SMEs) have been given a prominent role. SMEs are

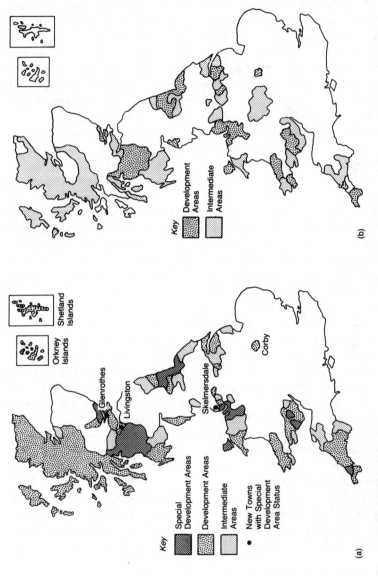

Figure 6 British Assisted Areas at (a) July 1984 and (b) November 1984. Source: official statistics

regarded not only as possible providers of large numbers of jobs in the depressed regions, but also as bastions of entrepreneurial values – places in which the enterprise culture can flourish.

This upbeat view of SMEs is a very recent one. In the 1960s and early 1970s, government policy systematically favoured mergers and take-overs in order to create larger firms. It was believed that large firms were needed in order to reap the benefits of economies of scale and to compete effectively with industrial giants from overseas.

Supporters of SMEs have argued that it is to small firms that the depressed areas must look for future job creation. Such jobs bring with them the advantage of being in locally owned companies with a stronger commitment to the local area than a large multinational company would have. In addition, it is argued that SMEs can help to *diversify* the structure of industry in an area, thereby helping to overcome an over-dependence on one industry (such as chemicals).

SMEs are believed to be very flexible and quick to adapt to changing circumstances. Some would also argue that their innovation perform-ance is better than in larger firms, pointing to the heavy dependence on 'high tech' of small firms in biotechnology and information technology.

Small-firm enthusiasts go further still and argue that SMEs are *vital* in that they stimulate intense competition in an area, forcing even the largest firms to adopt competitive attitudes and practices. Some supporters even argue that small firms have better industrial relations and offer a better working environment for their employees.

The foregoing is a powerful array of arguments. If they could all be believed one would be left wondering why successive governments have neglected SMEs and favoured large firms. It should be noted, however, that there is a surprising paucity of information about SMEs, and until recently there has been very little systematic research on their perform-ance. This has made it difficult to test the various claims made by those who vociferously support a regional policy designed to stimulate the small firms sector.

It is clear from the admittedly limited statistics on SMEs that traditional regional policy was mistaken in its neglect of the SME sector. This neglect was, in part, unintentional. The emphasis on manufacturing firms inevitably meant that regional subsidies tended automatically to end up in large firms. This would not have been true if regional policy had also been targeted at **service industries**, which are dominated by SMEs. The switch of regional policy towards service sector firms will in itself draw regional policy away from large firms towards SMEs.

Even in manufacturing, however, the neglect of small firms cannot be

Table 15 New firm birth rates in British regions, 1980–83

Region	Business start-ups per 1000 employees 1980–83	Percentage increase in the number of businesses 1979–83
South West	56.0	11.7
East Anglia	53.0	12.4
South East	53.2	14.9
East Midlands	42.6	12.0
West Midlands	39.3	11.3
Yorkshire/Humberside	38.5	8.5
North West	38.4	6.6
North	30.8	8.6
Wales	44.3	9.1
Scotland	32.1	9.7
Great Britain	44.6	11.6

Source: Ganguly, P., 'Business starts and stops: UK county analysis 1980', *British Business*, 18 January 1985.

defended. SMEs with under 100 employees account for over 20 per cent of all *manufacturing* jobs in the UK. This is simply too large a sector to ignore. Moreover, the UK's small firms sector is under-developed compared with the equivalent sector in other EEC countries. The UK appears to be out of line with her competitors, which suggests a potential for growth in the SME sector.

Another encouraging feature concerning SMEs has been the surge in birth rates of *new* SMEs. Table 15 shows rates of new firm formation by region, for the period 1980/83, spanning the worst years of the severe recession of the early 1980s. The rapid rate of new firm formation at a time of a major economic downturn is very impressive, particularly as these new small firms are the 'seed corn' from which the industrial giants of the future will one day grow.

Sceptics of a regional policy based on SMEs strike a more pessimistic note. They argue that figures such as those presented in Table 15 are not surprising – new firm birth rates always rise in a recession, only to fall back later. Redundancy often pushes individuals into founding their own businesses (particularly where big redundancy payments are given and where lots of spare second-hand machinery and factory premises are lying idle). There is also the problem that the high birth rate has been accompanied by a high **mortality rate**. As many as one-half of new firms die within five years, and the survivors grow only slowly.

To make matters worse, the depressed regions do not seem to be good places to set up a new small firm. Most of the depressed regions have low rates of new firm formation (see Table 15). The reasons are complex; but it is not too difficult to see that depressed regions have few of the characteristics helpful for the successful establishment of any new firm: a buoyant local economy, the ready availability of highly educated persons, a pool of budding entrepreneurs with managerial experience in other SMEs, and a high proportion of owner-occupied housing (since most new firms are financed by a second mortgage on the founder's own home). To rely on SMEs thriving in the hostile environment of a depressed region is a very high risk strategy.

Conclusion

The new regional policy emerging in Britain is less expensive than its predecessor and radically different. There is now much greater emphasis on helping service sector industries such as finance, insurance and tourism. Small firms and innovation have been allocated much greater roles in renewing the depressed areas, while older types of financial help – such as investment subsidies for manufacturing firms – still exist. Much more selectivity is now applied by civil servants in allocating the available funds.

These are revolutionary changes. They are also very high risk changes. Most have never been tried on such a scale before. Their introduction appears to have been preceded by surprisingly little evaluation, analysis and forecasting.

KEY WORDS

Special Areas	Cost per job
Job creation	Enterprise culture
Inward investment	Technological innovations
Location controls	Service industries
Investment subsidies	Mortality rate
Assisted Areas	

Reading list

S. Bazen and T. Thirwell, *Deindustrialization,* Heinemann Educational, 1989, Chapter 6.

Glaister, K., *The Entrepreneur,* Heinemann Educational, 1989, Chapters 6 and 7.

Moore, B., Rhodes, J. and Tyler, P., *The Effects of Government Regional Economic Policy,* HMSO, London, 1986.

Wigley, P., 'The impact of technical innovation', *Economic Review*, September 1986.

Essay topics

1. What were the main characteristics of traditional regional policy? Was traditional regional policy appropriate for its era?
2. How effective was traditional regional policy in creating jobs, encouraging inward investment in the depressed areas, and in providing value-for-money for taxpayers?
3. What are the main advantages and disadvantages of a regional policy relying heavily on small and medium-sized enterprises?

Data Response Question 5

Business life expectancy

Most new businesses have a very short life expectancy. Table 16 presents statistics of the lifespans of new businesses (those registering for VAT purposes) which were set up between 1974 and 1982. Drawing on the data provided by this table, answer the following questions.

1. Using graph paper, plot – for each industrial sector in turn – 'percentage of businesses' on the vertical axis against 'lifespan' on the horizontal axis.
2. (a) What is the *mean* lifespan of the firms in *each* industrial sector? (b) What is the *mean* lifespan when *all* industries are taken together? (c) What is the *modal* lifespan when *all* industries are taken together? [Note: the *mean* lifespan is obtained for any one industry as follows. Multiply the mid-points of the lifespans (i.e. 3, 9, 15, etc.) in the initial column by the corresponding percentages in the relevant industry column, add up all the answers thus obtained, and divide by 100. The *modal* lifespan is the most common one.]
3. In which industries do you think it would be best to start a new business?
4. What do you think might be the reasons for the very short lifespan in all industries?
5. Overall, some 58.8 per cent of businesses set up between 31 January 1974 and 31 January 1982 were still in existence on 1 February 1982. Can we safely assume that most of these are now viable and will go on surviving into the foreseeable future?
6. What are the implications of your analysis of the data in Table 16 for the government's newest regional policy targeted on small firms, services and innovation? How could the government improve the existing new firm survival rates?

Table 16 Lifespans of businesses registered for VAT between 1974 and 1982, by industry

Lifespan (months)	Agriculture	Production	Construction	Transport	Wholesale	Retail	Finance, property & professional services	Catering	Motor trades	Other services	Total (%)	Total (number)
0– 6	8.0	12.4	12.2	12.9	14.2	9.0	8.5	8.1	13.7	10.9	10.8	61 061
6– 12	10.6	14.9	15.5	16.6	16.2	14.6	13.4	14.0	16.8	15.1	15.0	84 359
12– 18	13.4	15.0	15.4	15.3	15.5	15.3	15.9	15.4	15.8	15.2	15.3	86 421
18– 24	11.8	12.5	12.3	11.9	11.9	13.3	13.4	13.3	12.4	12.6	12.7	71 526
24– 30	11.3	10.3	10.5	9.9	9.9	11.3	10.7	11.3	10.0	10.5	10.7	60 080
30– 36	8.9	8.0	8.1	7.9	7.6	8.8	8.4	9.0	7.5	8.1	8.3	46 770
36– 42	8.0	6.6	6.4	6.1	6.2	7.1	6.8	7.3	6.0	6.8	6.7	37 968
42– 48	6.3	4.9	4.8	4.7	4.5	5.3	5.3	5.4	4.3	4.8	5.0	28 250
48– 54	5.4	4.0	3.9	3.7	3.7	4.1	4.7	4.3	3.6	4.1	4.1	22 979
54– 60	4.7	2.9	2.7	2.9	2.8	3.1	3.5	3.1	2.7	3.0	3.0	17 037
60– 66	3.5	2.4	2.3	2.3	2.3	2.5	2.9	2.7	2.1	2.6	2.5	14 043
66– 72	2.7	2.0	1.8	1.7	1.6	1.8	2.2	2.0	1.6	2.0	1.9	10 658
72– 78	2.1	1.5	1.5	1.4	1.2	1.4	1.8	1.6	1.3	1.6	1.5	8 348
78– 84	1.3	1.0	1.0	0.9	0.9	1.0	1.1	1.0	0.9	1.0	1.0	5 590
84– 90	1.0	0.7	0.7	0.8	0.7	0.7	0.7	0.7	0.6	0.8	0.7	4 032
90– 96	0.5	0.5	0.5	0.5	0.4	0.4	0.5	0.4	0.4	0.5	0.4	2 523
96–102	0.4	0.3	0.3	0.2	0.2	0.2	0.3	0.2	0.2	0.3	0.2	1 391
102–108	0.1	0.1	0.1	0.1	0.1	0.0	0.1	0.0	0.1	0.1	0.1	364
A	13 606	49 364	84 647	33 165	44 793	132 940	33 228	60 245	34 229	77 183	100	563 400
B	62 938	80 495	132 241	37 392	68 885	163 142	58 682	77 284	46 737	109 581		837 377

Notes: (A) = number of businesses registered since January 1974 and deregistered before 31 January 1982.
(B) = number of businesses registered since January 1974 and still trading on 31 December 1982.

Source: Ganguly, P., and Bannock, G., *UK Small Business Statistics and International Comparisons*, Harper and Row, London, 1985.

Chapter Six

Regional problems and policies: the European dimension

'*What we are contemplating is a strategic predicament of Wagnerian proportions. . . . any significant positive growth rate . . . will now cause the current account deficit to deteriorate further, while to get an improvement probably requires that growth ceases altogether or even that output falls. I used to think the answer . . . lay in some kind of protection. However, our greater commitment to Europe seems to rule this out. Hence the only solution would appear to be the active exploitation of all the opportunities now offered by the EC in terms of regional policy, very broadly defined, as well as monetary and fiscal cooperation.*' Wynne Godley, Professor of Economics at the University of Cambridge, *The Guardian*, 5 July 1989

A watershed in European Community regional policy

The above quotation indicates vividly that EC regional policy has finally come of age. Economic integration of the member states has been given a great fillip by the 1987 **Single Europe Act**. The year 1992 has been designated as a key year in the process of sweeping away the last of the barriers to trade. The aim is ambitious – a **single internal market**. This 'Europe without frontiers' would encompass a market of 320 million consumers and would command one-fifth of all world trade.

The EC, of course, is already well on the way towards full economic integration. Formal **tariffs and quotas** on internal trade have been removed. The 1992 process seeks the removal of three other types of trade barrier:

1. Cost-increasing barriers
Delays and bureaucracy at frontier customs posts, and the costly effects of different national rules and standards for goods, are examples of this type of barrier to free trade.

2. Market-entry restrictions
Many member state governments deliberately favour local firms when

orders are being placed. Orders for defence equipment are a good example. Complex rules often prevent foreigners from taking control of any individual country's companies. These and other sorts of market-entry restrictions are intended to be abolished after 1992.

3. Market-distorting practices
Market distortions arise as a result of government price controls, taxes and subsidies and as a result of collusion among firms. All are targets for the 1992 deadline for reform.

Removing all of these barriers cannot, of course, be achieved by 1992. In many respects, 1992 marks only the start of the process. The commitment has, however, been made. A glance down the list of barriers to be removed under the **1992 proposals** reveals the extent of the loss of power of member governments to protect their depressed regions. The preferential placing of government contracts with depressed area firms would also be frowned upon.

More seriously still, beyond 1992 loom even more radical reforms. Jacques Delors, President of the European Commission, has introduced proposals for a much faster movement towards the ultimate in economic integration – **Economic and Monetary Union** (EMU). These proposals – hotly contested by Mrs Thatcher – envisage a single central bank and a single EC currency, and member states would effectively cede major fiscal and monetary policy powers to the European Parliament. Beyond these proposals lies an even more startling possibility – political union with a federal system of government.

Step-by-step the member states' sovereign powers are being weakened. With each step the power of the British government to act unilaterally to protect the depressed regions of Britain is being eroded. EC regional policy is being erected as a replacement for these waning powers.

The real challenges after 1992
The current pattern of regional problems in the EC is shown in Figure 7, which gives each regions' GDP per capita. By and large, the depressed regions lie on the *periphery* of the EC. The most prosperous regions lie at the geographical *centre*. This is no coincidence. The **economic integration** which has already occurred in the EC appears to have favoured the central regions. The 1992 reforms and progress towards EMU can be expected to continue this 'centralizing' process.

The ways in which individual regions are affected by EC integration are poorly understood. They are certainly very complex. Successful

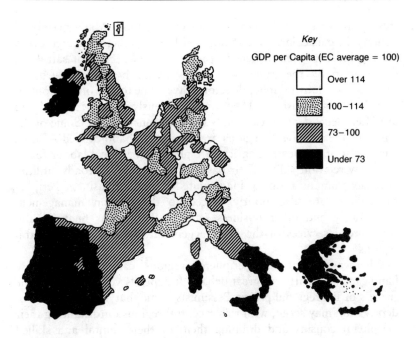

Key

GDP per Capita (EC average = 100)

☐	Over 114
▦	100–114
▨	73–100
■	Under 73

Figure 7 Regional gross domestic product per capita, 1985. Source: official EC statistics

integration leads to faster growth, the benefits of which will eventually filter down to everyone, wherever they live. Against this, however, must be set the effects of what is going to be an immense **supply-side shock**. The completion of the internal market will mean that customers will buy from the cheapest suppliers, wherever they are in the EC. Competitive and efficient industries will thrive; uncompetitive industries will decline. All regions will feel this supply-side shock: some industries will decline while others will expand (if the law of comparative advantage is to be believed). Substantial movements of labour and capital from one industry to another and from one region to another will be required.

Specialization should mean greater efficiency. With a market of 320 million potential customers the opportunities to exploit economies of scale will be immense. This confers an important benefit on central regions. Firms wishing to serve the whole EC market can reach their customers more easily if they are located near to one of the major road or rail hubs on the rapidly improving EC transport system.

To make matters worse, there are in the Community more than a few **structurally backward regions**, many of which will therefore begin this battle for survival from a very weak position. Many peripheral regions, in particular, have antiquated business sectors geared up to serving local markets which, in the past, have been kept safe from competition by the 'tyranny of distance' or by cunning frontier regulations. Many peripheral regions have come to rely on only one or two **declining industries**. They are dangerously over-specialized and are often dependent on externally owned branch plants. Some of the worst of the peripheral regions are even more handicapped – often barely out of the peasant agriculture phase. Their local labour forces have few relevant skills. Their basic infrastructure (of roads, utilities and telecommunications) is inadequate for modern business. Peripheral regions are also poorly placed to draw upon management consultancy and other business services. The major financial and commercial services of the EC are generally located in the central regions.

Whether or not the peripheral regions can overcome these handicaps is a matter of great debate. It depends very heavily on the success of EC regional policy. Pessimists argue that a **vicious circle of deprivation** may set in, with richer central regions outdistancing their peripheral cousins and draining them of their capital and skilled labour. EC regional disparities have been worsening in recent years. Unless action is taken this could get much worse.

The prospect of economic and monetary union raises even more difficulties for the peripheral regions. Some EC member states are virtually depressed regions in their own right – countries such as Greece, Portugal and the Republic of Ireland. Such countries can, at present, protect their citizens' jobs by allowing their currencies to depreciate in value against the currencies of other EC countries. They also manipulate their domestic tax, government spending and monetary policy to protect their own economies. EMU will change all this. A single currency (or even just 'locked' exchange rates) will remove the devaluation option. Loss of monetary policy powers to a single central EC bank and fiscal policy powers to Brussels will expose the weaker economies to the chill winds of competition. In such circumstances, EC regional policy becomes the vital lifeline: the means of giving the weaker economies a breathing space to get their houses in order. No longer would EC regional policy be an expensive luxury; it would be vital to the success of the EC's entire mission.

A new EC regional policy for 1992

The recognition that regional policy has a strategic role to play in the 1992 process has led to a radical reform of the existing EC regional policy. A whole series of new regulations came into force on 1 January 1989. The new EC 'regional policy for 1992' consists of three main parts.

The structural funds

These consist of the European Regional Development Fund (ERDF), the European Social Fund (ESF) and the 'Guidance' section of the European Agricultural Guidance and Guarantee Fund (EAGGF). All three of these funds have existed for many years.

The ERDF has existed since 1975 as the EC's main regional policy instrument. It is used to give grants and interest rebates on loans to industrial and infrastructure projects in depressed regions.

The ESF has long operated with a deliberate regional bias, financing many different types of labour market policies (e.g. training schemes and worker mobility schemes).

The Guidance section of the EAGGF is designed to assist rural areas by helping the farming industry to adapt, restructure and reinvest, and to stimulate new types of industry in areas where agricultural employment is in decline.

While none of the three **Structural Funds** is new, under the reformed regional policy they are to be substantially expanded.

Other EC institutions harnessed to the regional policy effort

Of particular importance are the European Investment Bank (EIB) and the European Coal and Steel Community (ECSC). The EIB has existed since 1958 and has always operated with a regional bias – channelling loans, usually on very good terms, to firms and public authorities in depressed areas.

The ECSC dates from 1952. Simply by virtue of the two industries with which it is involved, its activities (e.g. loans, grants, retraining and rehousing workers) have greatly helped certain depressed regions, many of which are in Britain.

Coordination of policy initiatives

The EC has known from the start that, for its regional policy to be a success, it would have to work closely both with the member states (each having its own regional policy), and with regional and local development organizations. It would therefore be ultimately responsible for **coordination initiatives.**

Under its **competition policy** regulations, for example, the EC has legal powers to monitor and control the types of assistance each member state can provide through its own regional policy. Ceilings are put on the amount of financial help which can be given to firms in each region of the EC. These are designed to prevent more prosperous member states from using regional subsidies to bid 'competitively' (that is, unfairly) for projects which would otherwise go to depressed regions in poorer countries.

Coordination is also encouraged by the EC in various other ways. Member states must submit **regional development plans** and progress reports. For its part, the EC undertakes continuous regional research, prepares regular periodic reports on regional problems in the EC, and uses these reports to draw up sets of priorities and guidelines for member states. The EC also tries to ensure that all of its component parts act in unison when tackling regional problems. To help in this process, all major EC policy changes are subject to a regional **impact assessment** which evaluates the likely effects on the depressed areas and tries to circumvent any adverse effects *before* they happen.

More about the Structural Funds

Important though the initiatives to coordinate policies are, it is the Structural Funds (SFs) which will dominate EC regional policy in the years to come; and as already stated, the ERDF is the key fund for regional policy purposes.

The importance of the SFs has been guaranteed by the decision to double the resources (in real terms) by 1993. The money available will rise in stages from 7.7 billion ECUs (£5.0 billion) in 1988 to 14.1 billion ECUs (£9.2 billion at 1988 price levels) in 1993. This is a major expansion, although it should be borne in mind that this money is to be shared between all twelve member states, and that in 1989 the agriculture price support policy of the EC was itself allocated 27 billion ECUs. Regional policy has a long way to go before it catches up with EC financial support to farmers.

It must also be borne in mind that the SFs are concerned not only with regional policy objectives but also with various *non-regional objectives*; for example, eliminating youth unemployment wherever it occurs in the EC. Not all of the £9.2 billion in 1993 will go to the depressed areas. In fact, only *three* of the six objectives of the Structural Funds are explicitly regional. These are:

- *The development of structurally backward regions* (Objective 1). As Figure 8 shows, the low-income regions which fall into this category stretch in a broad swathe through the Mediterranean part of the EC, and encompass the whole of Ireland. It is expected that 80 per cent of ERDF expenditures will be directed at these regions.

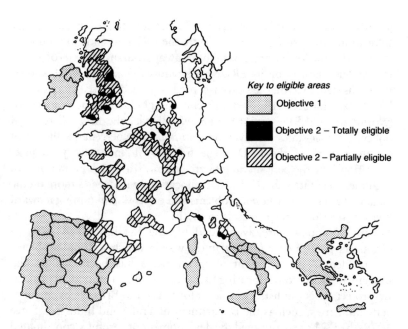

Figure 8 The 1989 map of EC assisted areas: areas eligible under Objectives 1 and 2 discussed in the text. Source: official EC statistics

- *The conversion of regions of industrial decline* (Objective 2). Regions of industrial decline are the main type of depressed region in Britain, where these regions contain some 20 million people.
- *The development of rural areas*. This is a very small category. Less than £600 million will be available under this heading for the whole of the EC in 1993. In Britain, the Scottish Highlands, and parts of Wales, Devon, Cornwall, Dumfries and Galloway will be eligible for assistance under the rural areas scheme.

Figure 8 is an historic document, being the first map *ever* of EC assisted areas. Until now, the EC has been forced to rely on the assisted area maps drawn up by each member state for their individual regional policies.

Efforts to direct the use of funds

The EC has taken the opportunity presented by the need to reform regional policy as part of the 1992 process to introduce a number of other sought-after changes. Firstly, a determined attempt is to be made to increase the proportion of ERDF assistance going to industrial investment projects rather than for general infrastructure (e.g. roads, drainage) in the depressed areas. In 1987, over 91 per cent of ERDF expenditure went to infrastructure projects, a figure the ERDF intends to reduce.

Secondly, the EC has tried hard to get away from the concept of a *juste retour* ('just return') on its ERDF expenditures. Prior to 1979, member states insisted that they be given a predetermined share, or quota, of ERDF expenditures. This requirement was gradually eroded in major reforms to the ERDF in 1979 and 1984. Under the new EC regional policy, member states are given only an *indicative* percentage allocation for their share of the ERDF. The first set of 'indicative percentage allocations' for the period 1989/93 are given in Table 17. From now on, each member state's share of ERDF allocations will depend more on the actual severity of its regional problems and on its skill in putting forward regional development proposals to the EC.

Thirdly, and as already alluded to, the EC has taken steps to encourage greater *coordination* in the way in which regional problems are tackled. A key element in this process has been the gradual movement away from allocating ERDF money on an individual project-by-project basis (on lists of projects forwarded to Brussels by member state ministries, such as the Department of Trade and Industry). Since 1979, the EC has encouraged the development of carefully coordinated *programmes* (rather than project-by-project assistance) as a basis for allocating ERDF resources. A programme is a coordinated package of investment projects and policy initiatives designed to run for several

Table 17 Indicative percentage allocations of ERDF funds: 1989–93

Country	Development of structurally backward regions	Conversion of regions of industrial decline	Development of rural areas
Belgium	0.0	4.3	1.2
Denmark	0.0	0.4	0.7
Germany	0.0	8.9	27.5
Greece	6.2	0.0	0.0
Spain	32.6	20.7	7.2
France	2.1	18.3	37.2
Republic of Ireland	5.4	0.0	0.0
Italy	24.5	6.3	16.4
Luxembourg	0.0	0.2	0.1
Netherlands	0.0	2.6	2.2
Portugal	17.5	0.0	0.0
United Kingdom	1.7	38.3	7.5
	100	100	100

Source: European Communities Commission, *Official Journal*, 1989.

years and designed to attack a specific type of regional problem. A good example is the Textile Areas Programme, one of the first introduced. Areas affected by the decline of textile industries have received special ERDF help. Programmes are designed to draw in other EC funds (e.g. from the European Social Fund) and involve member states and local agencies as well as the ERDF.

Since 1984, 'programme' assistance has grown rapidly while 'project' assistance has declined. Two distinctive types of programme have been used: **Community Programmes** and **National Programmes of Community Interest** (NPCIs). Community Programmes are initiated by the EC and encompass the whole Community. A good example is STAR, a programme designed to improve the provision of advanced telecommunications services in depressed regions right across the EC. NCPIs are initiated by member states and are confined to that one country. By the end of 1988, 78 NPCIs had been approved. A good example is the Mersey Basin Programme, designed to clean up the Mersey river system and renew industry and infrastructure in the area.

The development of coordinated programmes should be stimulated by the recent reforms to EC regional policies. Member states are having to develop new regional plans to which the EC will respond by drawing up a **Community Support Framework**. These documents will provide a framework within which specific integrated programmes can be developed drawing together the activities of the Structural Funds, the EIB, the ECSC, member states and local development organizations. The EC already has considerable expertise in developing this type of integrated programme approach. Integrated Mediterranean programmes, for example, have existed for many years and have been used to focus EC help on the severely disadvantaged regions in the south of the EC. On a smaller scale, Integrated Development Operations have been used to attack inner-city problem areas, beginning in Naples and Belfast. How successful all of these complex coordinated programmes will prove to be remains to be seen. *What cannot be doubted is that effective coordination of regional policy is long overdue.*

A fourth long-sought-after reform of EC regional policy has been the concentration of assistance where it is most needed. The recent reforms represent a major step forward in this respect since 80 per cent of the ERDF funds will go to the structurally backward regions. This is bad news for the UK, which contains only Northern Ireland in this category. On the other hand, the UK *does* have several regions of *industrial decline* as well as several rural areas eligible for assistance. Clearly, then, the UK will gain from the doubling of the size of the SFs by 1993, but will lose out by only having one region in the backward

Table 18 Allocations from the European Regional Development Fund, 1975–88 (millions of ECUs; 1 ECU is about 65p)

	Project assistance	Programme assistance	Studies	Total 1975–88	1988
(a) *By member state*					
Belgium	174	27	2.0	203	24
Denmark	166	7	6.1	179	10
Germany	849	49	0.2	898	84
Greece	2185	250	0.2	2435	328
Spain	1948	27	0.0	1975	674
France	2537	262	12.0	2811	306
Ireland	1157	144	0.7	1302	148
Italy	7753	112	21.5	7887	939
Luxembourg	15	2	0.0	17	1
Netherlands	230	11	0.2	241	20
Portugal	1083	95	0.5	1179	410
UK	**4621**	**374**	**10.1**	**5005**	**465**
(b) *By UK region*					
North	728	47	0.9	776	105
Yorks/Humberside	379	0	0.7	380	16
East Midlands	70	0	0.9	71	5
South West	219	0	0.4	220	16
West Midlands	286	22	0.2	308	38
North West	540	105	1.0	646	53
Wales	715	54	1.7	771	94
Scotland	1042	142	1.5	1185	76
N. Ireland	520	0	1.1	522	62
Multi-regional	120	5	1.8	127	1
Totals	**4619**	**375**	**10.2**	**5005**	**466**

Notes: (1) The figures are *allocations* and not payments. Payments lag allocation by varying amounts of time. (2) Figures refer to the period up to and including the tenth allocation, 1988.
Source: European Communities, *Information Memo p-1*, 10 Jan. 1989.

regions category. Overall, however, the reforms should ensure that more money is directed at the worst-off areas of the EC. Table 18 shows how much ERDF help UK regions have had since 1975.

Conclusion

The Single Europe Act and proposals for economic and monetary union have led to a fundamental change in emphasis in regional policy in Britain. EC regional policy operations in Britain have grown steadily since 1975. This has coincided with a decline in the British government's own regional policy efforts. Between now and 1992, EC regional policy will be greatly strengthened and radically reformed. The depressed regions of Britain will look increasingly to Brussels for help. They will need to. European economic integration poses a serious threat to the well-being of the depressed areas. It also offers considerable opportunities for those willing to sieze them.

KEY WORDS

Single Europe Act
Single internal market
Tariffs and quotas
1992 proposals
Economic and monetary
  union
Economic integration
Supply-side shock
Structurally backward
  regions
Declining industries
Vicious circle of deprivation

Structural Funds
Coordination initiatives
Competition policy
Regional development
  plans
Impact assessment
Community Programmes
National Programmes of
  Community Interest
Community Support
  Framework

Reading list

Cecchini, P., *The European Challenge, 1992: The Benefits of a Single Market*, Wildwood House, London, 1988.

R. Levačić, *Supply Side Economics*, Heinemann Educational, 1989.

McDonald, F., 'The single market: the likely impact on the UK economy', *British Economy Survey*, Spring, 1989.

McKenzie, G. and Venables, T. 'The economics of 1992', *Economic Review*, May 1989.

Swann, D., *The Economics of the Common Market*, Pelican, 1988.

Essay topics

1. What main benefits are likely to flow to Britain as a result of the Single Europe Act in 1992? Will all regions benefit?
2. Which parts of Britain will benefit from the recent reforms to EC regional policy? Are Britain's regional problems different from those of other EC countries?
3. Should the British government cease to have a regional policy of its own and let Brussels take over all regional policy?

Data Response Question 6

EC regional aid

Not everyone is wholeheartedly in favour of the great increase in EC regional policy expenditure envisaged under the 1992 proposals, as the accompanying article from *The Economist* of 15 July 1989 shows. Read the article and then answer the following questions.

1. What arguments might the 'British officials' referred to in the article put forward to defend their view that there is no need whatsoever for an EC role in regional policy?
2. What counter-arguments might the EC's own officials put forward to defend their increased regional policy powers?
3. List the main additional powers the EC has gained as a result of the reforms to EC regional policy?
4. Why is DG16 'constantly scraping against DG4'?
5. What is meant by the term 'additionality' and why is it such a problem for EC regional policy?
6. What reasons lie behind the suggestion that we can expect further rapid growth in EC spending on regional policy in the years *after* 1993?

The budget-buster of the 1990s?

The EEC is becoming less of an agricultural protection racket and more of a regional-aid fund. As our Brussels correspondent reports, spending on the regions is growing faster than any other area of the Community's budget

The Community's regional policy is the flip side to its single-market project. Southern Europeans feared that their poorer regions would wilt under the ferocity of post-1992 competition. So they accepted the single market only on condition that regional aid was stepped up.

Not everybody is convinced that the Community will now get its regional

policy right. In Britain, in particular, some officials still doubt the need for any EEC role at all. Critics are concerned about the powers the Commission has gained. In the past a management committee of officials from the member-states vetted the aid payments; this has now been turned into a toothless advisory committee. And while each country used to receive a quota of the available aid, the proportions are now merely indicative. Britain can expect to receive about 39% of money going to declining industrial areas, but could get less if it does not listen to the commission's comments on the programmes it puts forward. The commission cannot force a member-state to amend a plan, but it can deny money to measures it does not like.

The commission has also set aside up to 15% of the regional fund for its own pet priorities. It is currently financing EEC programmes to aid telecommunications and energy conservation in backward regions. As the commission's power has grown, so has its manpower. Since March 1986 the staff of DG16, the regional directorate, has grown from 180 to nearly 300.

So far the regional fund has seemed free of the fraud that has bedevilled the EEC's spending on agriculture. A more serious problem is waste and incompetence. Portugal, Greece and Italy, for example, have left unspent some of the money given them. The commission says a new rule that stops money being carried over from one year to another has cut the unspent portion of the regional fund from 12% to 1%. Prompted by Britain, the commission has tightened controls over the regional fund: it now carries out spot checks on project sites and is strengthening its anti-fraud inspectorate, while member-states must audit and monitor the money they receive.

DG 16 is constantly scraping against DG4, the competition directorate, which tries to limit state aid to industry. While DG16 is the territory of a British socialist commissioner, Mr Bruce Millan, DG4 is under a British Tory, Sir Leon Brittan. Rules on the permitted levels of subsidy for different regions generally preserve a fragile truce between the two directorates. Up to 45% of an investment in Portugal can be subsidised, but no more than 10% in West Germany.

A row between the commission and Britain is brewing over "additionality". Under the new aid regime, EEC money must be additional to cash that national governments had already agreed to spend – that is, EEC aid should not let governments get away with spending less. Britain's interpretation of this rule is loose: it reckons that it can replace its own commitments with EEC cash so long as an equivalent amount of government spending ultimately benefits the region concerned. This worries Mr Millan, who has already warned British ministers about additionality in Northern Ireland. He says that any country that tries to break the rules may find that EEC money is withheld.

The new regional policy has not yet had time to work, or fail. So for the moment those who doubt its usefulness are keeping quiet. But if the policy becomes tarred with waste or fraud, the sceptics will attack, and certainly oppose any increase in spending.

The structural funds' size has been fixed until 1993, but argument over how much to spend after that will start soon. Some north European countries, including West Germany, may back southern Europe and Ireland in calling for more regional aid. For if the backward countries' trade deficit with northern Europe grows ever worse, the alternative could be calls for protection or balance-of-payments loans from the EEC such as France received in 1982.

Progress towards monetary union will increase this pressure. The Delors report on monetary union points out that, since a single currency would deprive poorer countries of the ability to devalue, it could worsen their balance-of-payments difficulties. For Mr Jacques Delors, president of the commission and architect of the regional-policy reform, monetary union is inconceivable without a big increase in EEC aid for poorer regions.

Chapter Seven

Regional problems and policies: the local dimension

'. . . we have considerable sympathy with local authorities' concern to alleviate unemployment. But we are equally conscious that there are difficult underlying issues which have not yet been comprehensively addressed. These turn on . . . the role of the public sector as a whole in the promotion of the economy, the respective roles of different tiers of government and government agencies, and about competition for available resources between different regions.' Waddicombe Report (Command 9797), HMSO, 1986

The local dimension to regional issues

The ten **standard regions** of Britain are far from homogeneous. Each region is a patchwork of cities, towns and rural areas. Variations in economic well-being *within* each region greatly exceed variations *between* regions. Table 1 in Chapter 2 provides some evidence of the within-region variation in unemployment rates in Great Britain.

Nor is it just the level of unemployment which varies from place to place within each region. Other measures of economic well-being display similar wide variations. Moreover, when one looks closely at local areas within each region it becomes apparent that a huge variety of different *types* of regional problem exist. A region such as the North West, for example, contains within its borders several distinctive types of problem areas. Liverpool and Manchester have depressed inner-city areas with an explosive mixture of economic, social and ethnic problems. Other parts of the North West contain many dilapidated industrial towns which are struggling to find a new sense of direction. Along the coast lie holiday resorts dependent upon a tourist market which is oriented far more towards the Mediterranean sunspots than towards the beaches of Blackpool, Morecambe and Southport. Even prosperous regions have their problems – congestion, pollution and high property prices. Indeed, all British regions have their own specific regional problems – and this includes the prosperous south.

The diversity which underlies regional problems in Britain poses an immense challenge. How does one tackle a problem that is simultaneously both complex and constantly changing? The answer, of course, is to avoid rigidity. *Regional policy must be designed to avoid rigidity.* It must be flexible if it is to deal with problems of widely differing types and if it is to respond quickly to changing circumstances. *Over-centralization must also be avoided.* Regional policy must have a local dimension which reflects the diversity found at the local level. British regional policy was traditionally both tightly centralized and very rigidly applied. Sadly, there is little evidence that a coherent and carefully thought-out local 'arm' of regional policy is being developed.

The local delivery system for regional policy in Britain

The current **local delivery system** for regional policy is extraordinarily complex. In addition, there is also a problem of inconsistency from region to region. Scotland and Wales, for example, have a very different local delivery system from that of the English regions. Moreover, the system in Scotland differs from that in Wales. Throughout Britain the metropolitan areas have a different system from the rest. The Northern Ireland situation is even more distinctive – uniquely organized and completely different from the British regions.

At any one time in the British depressed regions, literally hundreds of different organizations are actively involved in promoting economic development initiatives. Not all of these are part of what has normally been regarded as 'regional' policy. Some are part of urban policy. Others are part of rural areas policy. Yet others are part of *national* policies designed to stimulate industry generally in all regions. The traditional boundaries between regional, urban, rural and other government policies have become very blurred in recent years.

The local delivery system for economic development policy in developed regions can best be described by grouping the various organizations involved into six broad levels of intervention.

European-level intervention

Mercifully, the EC does not have a bureaucracy which reaches down into the regions and local areas of the member states. EC regional policy is therefore forced to rely on national and local authorities to provide the delivery system. Applications for, and payments of, European Regional Development Fund assistance are, for example, administered by the Department of Trade and Industry (DTI) and by the Scottish and Welsh Offices in Britain.

National-level intervention

The role of the DTI, Scottish and Welsh Offices in delivering the British government's own regional policy has just been mentioned. The DTI has chosen to set up its own local delivery system in the *English* depressed regions via its regional offices. The need for a local delivery system is self-evident. What is not clear, however, is why the DTI chooses to work via its own offices rather than by simply utilizing the existing network of democratically elected local councils. After all, other ministries such as the Department of the Environment (DoE) actively employ local authorities as the main local delivery system for the government's *urban* policy.

Regional-level intervention

Britain is unusual in not having a set of elected regional governments. Most EC countries have quite powerful regional governments. In some federal countries (e.g. the USA, Canada and West Germany), the regional governments are very powerful indeed.

In the absence of elected regional governments or councils, a wide range of regional agencies have been set up by the government in order to stimulate regional economic development. The term used for these quasi-autonomous non-government organizations is **quangos**. These *quangos* include the **Highlands and Islands Development Board** (set up in 1965), the **Scottish Development Agency** (1976), the **Welsh Development Agency** (1976) and **Mid-Wales Development** (1976). All these agencies are very actively involved in development. In addition, they are actively involved in urban and rural policy, working closely with local councils in Scotland and Wales. For some functions, these regional agencies operate 'on the spot' through a network of their own local offices.

The regions in England do not have regional development agencies, although the government does part-finance a number of industrial promotion agencies in the Assisted Areas. Two English organizations operating at the local and regional level, however, are **English Estates** and the **Development Commission**. These *quangos* were set up and funded by the central government. English Estates builds and leases factories and provides serviced sites for firms, while the Development Commission has wide-ranging powers related to rural areas policy. The development of industry to replace jobs lost in farming is handled by the Commission for Small Industries in Rural Areas, a subsidiary of the Development Commission. English Estates and the Development Commission both use local councils to help to deliver their policies, but they also have their own networks of offices in local towns.

County-level intervention

Britain has a system of elected **county councils** (called 'regional authorities' in Scotland). In 1984, the *metropolitan* county councils were abolished leaving only the *shire* counties intact. County councils became actively involved in local economic development initiatives in the early 1980s and many remain heavily committed. **Enterprise Boards** were set up, for example, in Greater London, Lancashire, Merseyside, West Yorkshire and the West Midlands. Their purpose was (and still is) to provide loans, loan guarantees and equity for small and medium-sized companies. In addition, they provide assistance to develop new products and encourage the adoption of new technology, as well as aiding management buyouts of branch plants which are faced with closure. They also promote their own counties and provide premises for industry.

One of the main advantages of the Enterprise Boards is that they are able to bypass the normal bureaucratic processes of local authorities, thereby speeding up the decision-making process. They are also able to look towards the longer term for returns on their investment and to assess projects on social as well as economic grounds (since public funding is involved). Indeed, Greater London Enterprise (GLE) initially took a very radical view of its functions by putting social needs before profits. In particular, applications for support were assessed partly on the basis of solving social problems and promoting racial and sexual equality rather than simply on market-based criteria. Nevertheless, GLE has had to aim for commercial viability in order to survive. The abolition of the Greater London Council (GLC) in 1984, for example, led GLE to seek more private sector funds to replace those lost when Conservative borough councils withdrew their funding (see the Data Response Question at the end of this chapter).

District-level intervention

In addition to the county councils, Britain has over 350 **district councils** (called 'boroughs' in the metropolitan areas). These, too, became actively involved in local development initiatives in the 1980s. Typically, the councils set up separate companies and development agencies to handle initiatives on their behalf. These semi-independent organizations frequently draw heavily upon private sector companies for their expertise.

Community-level intervention

During the 1980s, local communities themselves took the initiative in helping to revive local businesses. These community-level initiatives now take many different forms. The most common are **Local Enterprise Agencies** and self-help 'clubs' of small firm entrepreneurs, much of the work being undertaken on a voluntary basis by local

Table 19 Expenditure on 'spatial' industrial policy in Britain, 1983–84

	£ million
European Economic Community	
European Regional Development Fund	46
European Investment Bank (loans)	92
European Coal and Steel Community (Conversion Loans)	52
Central Government	
Department of Trade and Industry	
Regional Development Grants	439
Regional Selective Assistance	82
Department of the Environment	
Urban Programme (industrial projects)	54
Enterprise Zones	40
Regional Organizations	
English Estates	41
Development Commission (industrial)	22
Scottish Development Agency	85
Welsh Development Agency	44
Highlands and Islands Development Board	27
Mid-Wales Development	7
Local government	
County councils	120
District councils	321

Notes: (1) Wherever possible, expenditure refers to expenditures actually incurred rather than to commitments made. (2) Expenditure on general infrastructure projects not directly tied to industrial development (such as roads and telecommunications) is excluded, as is expenditure on land reclamation and environmental improvements. This has been done to enable expenditures by different organizations to be directly compared. (3) Expenditure includes only deliberately geographically-discriminating assistance to industry. It includes the provision of sites and factories. (4) Local authority expenditure has been estimated from data supplied by the Chartered Institure of Public Finance and Accountancy. These estimates overstate the true expenditure made by local authorities since they include funds made available to councils by higher-order organizations (e.g. urban programme assistance from the Department of Environment and European Regional Development Fund grants).
Source: Armstrong, H. and Taylor J., *Regional Policy and the North-South Divide*, Employment Institute, London, 1988.

businessmen. Sometimes local-council or central-government money is put in on a **pump-priming** basis. Most of the help provided, as with the council's own help, is designed to foster the establishment and survival of *small* firms.

An early example of private support for local development initiatives is the St Helen's Trust, founded in 1978 by Pilkington's Glass in collaboration with other local private and public sector organizations. Its primary objective is to attack unemployment by creating an environment more favourable to the growth of business enterprise, particularly new small firms.

Trying to ascertain the relative importance of each of the six 'levels of intervention' set out above is an almost impossible task. Reliable statistics simply do not exist. Table 19 on the previous page presents the results of a first attempt at measuring the expenditures of the first five of the six levels of intervention. It is clear from the table that the British government no longer has a monopoly of industrial development policy in Britain; the regional and local dimension is now extremely strong.

The role of regional development agencies and local councils

Of all the regional and local organizations now involved in the delivery of regional policy in Britain, two stand out as being of particular importance – the regional development agencies in Scotland and Wales, and the local councils.

These organizations have taken the opportunity to try to fill the gap left by the cutbacks in the Department of Trade and Industry's regional policy spending. They have also proved to be highly innovative organizations by pioneering many of the new types of assistance and advice offered to small firms, and in helping firms to adopt technical innovations. In many ways they have proved to be the growth area of regional policy in the 1980s.

The Scottish and Welsh Development Agencies are the most powerful of the regional agencies (particularly the Scottish Development Agency, which is the largest of its kind in Europe). In 1987/88, for example, the Scottish Development Agency spent £145 million on new initiatives. As with the other agencies, this was partly financed by a **grant-in-aid** from the British government (£91.3 million in 1987/88 for the Scottish Development Agency). The remainder was raised by tapping other government sources (e.g. EC funds) or, increasingly, from their own earnings.

These 'own-earnings' take a variety of forms. The development agencies often buy shares in companies as a way of pumping funds into them. Annual dividend payments form one type of own-earnings. The agencies build, rent, buy and sell property, another source of own-earnings. They also make loans. As a result, interest payments and loan repayments form another source of own-earnings. Conceivably, one day the development agencies could become entirely *self-financing* and, possibly, privatized.

The regional development agencies are characterized by a very wide range of types of assistance. The Scottish Development Agency, for example, acquires and develops land for the building of factories, improves the environment, promotes Scotland for inward investment, and offers an advisory service to firms, particularly small firms.

It is interesting that county and district councils have developed a similarly wide range of initiatives for local development. Once again, small firms have been a favourite target group. They have been provided with grants, loans, premises, advertizing help and business advice.

The issue of 'who does what' in regional policy

With so many organizations now actively participating in regional policy the issue of 'who does what' has become one of paramount importance. There can be no return to a regional policy which is the monopoly of the central government. From a reading of Chapter 6, some might argue that EC regional policy is becoming too powerful and that greater efforts should be made to decentralize it.

The regional agencies and local councils can point to considerable successes. They would argue that their role is justified by their greater local knowledge and expertise. A powerful case can be made for active local participation in regional policy. Selective rather than automatic assistance is now the norm. Selectivity, to be successful, requires detailed local knowledge. Policies designed to help small firms, new technology and entrepreneurial skills are all characterized by a need for 'hands-on' assistance in the form of personal advice, carefully tailored packages of financial help, special types of factory units (small 'incubator' units) and the like. These all require a decentralized delivery system, even when financed by the central government or the EC.

Of course, one could not eliminate the British government or the EC entirely from regional policy and just leave it to regional agencies or local councils. At the end of the day, it will still be the taxpayers of the richer regions who must pay for help given to the poorer regions, and only the EC and member state governments can bring this about. The real issue is not *whether* the EC, British government, regional and local organizations should be involved, but rather *how* they should be involved. At present the situation is chaotic. The situation cries out for leadership – for each organization to be given a clear and distinctive role in the delivery system for regional policy. Until this occurs, considerable waste and mismanagement of scarce resources is likely to occur.

Conclusion

This chapter has described the involvement of local and regional organizations in regional policy. It has shown that a wide range of organizations, both public and private, are now actively engaged in stimulating regional economic development. Some of these are national or even supranational organizations, but many new institutions have been set up since the mid-1970s which operate at the local and regional levels.

One problem with this proliferation of organizations involved in regional development is the potential for a duplication of effort and hence wasted energy. Each organization is a law unto itself, even though their functions often overlap. The lack of coordination between this multiplicity of organizations could result in substantial waste. A possible solution to this problem – and to various other aspects of current regional policy – is the subject matter of the final chapter.

KEY WORDS

Standard regions	English Estates
Local delivery system	Development Commission
Highlands and Islands	County councils
Development Board	Enterprise Boards
Scottish Development	District councils
Agency	Local Enterprise Agencies
Welsh Development Agency	Grant-in-aid
Mid-Wales Development	Quangos
	Pump-priming

Reading list

A. Griffith and S. Wall, *Applied Economics,* 3rd ed., Longman, 1989, Chapter 19.

Essay topics

1. What role, if any, can company-financed local industrial development initiatives play in developing depressed areas? What problems might occur if such initiatives were greatly extended as a result of, say, additional government tax incentives for the firms involved?
2. What case could be made for extending regional development agencies to English regions, rather than confining them to Scotland and Wales? Should all English regions, including the South East, be allowed a development agency?
3. What are the 'pros and cons' of allowing local councils to operate their own local economic development initiatives?

Data Response Question 7

The future prospects for Greater London Enterprise

Read the accompanying article by Steve Eminton from the *Municipal Journal* of 10 March 1989 and answer the following questions.

1. London is normally regarded as one of the most prosperous places in Britain. Do you think that it actually *needs* its own local development agency?
2. What are the implications of a successful London development agency for the depressed regions of Britain? Could Greater London Enterprise make it harder to regenerate the depressed areas in the north of Britain?
3. What are the main activities of GLE? Could the firms obtain the same type of help in other ways?
4. Could GLE be privatized? Would privatization be a good idea?
5. GLE is threatened by a new Bill which could curtail all local council development initiatives. Should local councils be stopped from undertaking these types of policies? If local councils do not undertake this type of activity, who should?

Enterprising London

Greater London Enterprise is one of the most successful economic development arms of local government in the UK. But, with the government cracking down on local authority companies it is having to reshape its plans for the future.

The roots of the capital's main local authority economic development body go back to 1983, the year it was set up by the former Greater London

Council as a company under its control and ownership.

The word Board was dropped from the GLE's name in 1985 when its articles of association were changed prior to the abolition of the GLC. The company was allowed by the Department of the Environment to remain in existence and all London Boroughs and the City of London were invited to be members.

In the event 13 boroughs, all now Labour controlled, joined. Each had to pay for a £100 stake in the new company.

Now, the company believes its very existence is threatened by the proposals to cut local authority interest in companies that will be enacted through the Local Government and Housing Bill now at Commons committee stage. ... 'Our commercial flexibility would be severely diminished. The advantages we derive from the commercial manner in which we work would be lost.'

• • •

The alternative, says GLE, would be for the local authorities to relinquish their interest in GLE and sell the company to outside investors. 'GLE's assets, together with the skills of its staff and other goodwill, make us a saleable proposition. In this event, however, it is a matter of judgement how far the current range of activities and GLE's policy orientation towards smaller firms and the less economically developed parts of London, could and would be retained.' GLE's chairman is Tony Millwood, a Labour councillor with Hackney LBC.

• • •

Cllr Millwood is a firm supporter of the Government's belief that partnership approaches to a variety of subjects between local authorities and councils have a lot to offer, providing that the role the local authority can play is recognised. 'Nearly all of us nowadays are committed to a mixed economy with a substantial private sector. So, there are a range of questions as to how a local authority can contribute to the performance of the economy. Small firms, local authorities and central government all have within them locked up knowledge and skills. These are both very valuable for the economy.'

• • •

GLE is not market led, affirms Cllr Millwood, 'We target our efforts and attention to areas with economically disadvantaged groups. And we aim to work in those boroughs who are our members and also in those who invest in us, usually through pension funds, which includes Conservative authorities such as Wandsworth.

In fact, this relationship with the boroughs has taken a long time to build for they have guarded their own spheres of influence quite jealously', believes Cllr Millwood.

'This trust is now established and so we can develop our work which involves a division of labour and resources and other services. In identifying investment opportunities we have the benefit of local intelligence giving us an advantage over private capital. We are seeking to work in areas where the majority of private sector venture capital investors would not be impressed.'

Cllr Millwood lists five principal activities carried out by GLE:

1. The investment of risk capital in smaller and medium sized companies in amounts ranging from £50,000 to £500,000.
2. Provision of training for smaller businesses.

3. Provision of support and finance for new product developments.

4. Management of a property portfolio which offers factory premises and managed workspace for smaller and medium-sized businesses.

5. The GLE business incentive scheme which offers small soft loans to start-up businesses, targeted at ethnic minority entrepreneurs.

GLE has also set up a joint venture company with the private sector to carry out property development. GLE/Rosehaugh Developments PLC is to carry out a mixed development in Lewisham which will be worth about £60m.

GLE is in no danger of facing oblivion: the worst scenario would be its most successful parts being bought up by a merchant bank. But, this looks extremely unlikely. The way ahead for GLE is likely to be through the selling of shares in a new company with the existing local authority stakeholders having a minority interest. The existing company would remain but there would be a new parent company. The fixed assets, people and some money would go to the new company.

• • •

Cllr Millwood is firm in his belief that the work of GLE needs to continue and he cites firm support from both the Department of Trade and Industry and the Department of Employment for the company.

Its success in regenerating the economy of inner London boroughs is clear. Prime examples of success are the Lewisham project and venture capital business which is accelerating rapidly. The first three months of this year have seen as much invested as in the whole of 1988.

Chapter Eight

Regional policy in the 1990s: the way forward

'Regional policy is simply too valuable to the nation to be kept on such a parsimonious budget.'

This chapter presents our own proposals for reforming regional policy. In our view, not all the radical changes to regional policy that occurred during the 1980s have been welcome, and much more needs to be done if regional disparities are to be tackled effectively and efficiently during the 1990s.

One of our main criticisms of the latest reforms is the reduction in regional policy spending in real terms. This fall in **real regional policy expenditure** was inevitable during the early 1980s owing to the **nationwide recession** – since manufacturing investment fell sharply during 1979–81 and recovered only slowly during subsequent years. The recovery of investment in the second half of the 1980s, however, did not lead to a corresponding increase in *real* regional policy expenditure, mainly because of changes to the *type* of subsidy being offered. The automatic **Regional Development Grant** introduced in 1972 was amended in 1984 such that it became tied to the number of jobs created. The subsequent abolition of this grant in 1988 meant that all investment grants became discretionary and were therefore under the direct control of the government. The main reason was to make regional policy expenditure more cost-effective and to keep this expenditure within very strict limits. In our view, the abolition of the revised Regional Development Grant was a serious mistake which needs to be rectified.

There is also considerable scepticism about the likely effectiveness of several of the newer forms of regional policy introduced during the 1980s. This particularly applies to the faith which the government has in the ability of small and medium-sized firms (**SMEs**) to revive the fortunes of the most depressed areas. It is essential to evaluate these newer policies carefully so that the regional policy package can be made thoroughly effective.

Before explaining our proposals for reforming regional policy, it is important to draw attention to the considerable importance of **macroeconomic factors** in determining regional disparities. Historical experience clearly shows that regional disparities in employment opportunities have a strong tendency to *fall* when the economy is expanding rapidly – and to *increase* when the economy is moving into a slump. As Chapter 2 showed, regional unemployment disparities are at their greatest when *national* unemployment is at its highest, and the disparities shrink as national unemployment falls. Taking this one step further, long-run trends indicate that national unemployment will only fall if the annual growth of output *exceeds* 2.6 per cent. Strong national output growth is therefore required if the north–south divide is to be significantly reduced.

It is our contention that regional policy can help to bring about the stronger national growth which is so essential to the well-being of the most depressed regions. If economic growth is concentrated in the south, the British economy will inevitably run into severe inflationary problems as bottlenecks are encountered. Governments fear inflation more than any other economic problem, and the emergence of inflationary pressures causes them to use restrictive monetary and fiscal policy in order to reduce these pressures. The inevitable outcome is an economic recession – the old problem of **stop-go**.

There is now considerable evidence that the British economy is once again facing a serious inflationary problem. After several years of steady growth, the South East has yet again emerged as Britain's inflation-leader. Bottlenecks have been encountered in both the housing market and the labour market. House-price inflation which began in the South East has now spread to all parts of Britain. The same is happening to wage costs.

The government's response to these inflationary pressures has been to pull ever more tightly on the monetary reins. The initial response was a more restrictive monetary regime as the base interest rate was raised dramatically over a period of just a few months. If this fails to curb demand sufficiently, interest rates may be raised even further and government spending plans curtailed. These restrictions are an inevitable consequence of the government's own view that inflation is the 'judge and jury' of the success of its economic policies. Zero inflation is still the number-one target – in spite of an inflation rate approaching 8 per cent.

If these restrictive measures result in an economic downturn, it will be the north which will once again suffer the most. This is a powerful argument for strengthening regional policy, which should be seen not as a luxury to be enjoyed in good times but as an essential accompaniment to promoting sound and sustained growth. By spreading development and preventing the excessive geographical concentration of growth, regional policy can help to prevent the emergence of inflationary 'hot-spots' in the economy.

Our own ideas for strengthening regional policy are based upon four main proposals.

Proposal 1: Regional policy expenditure should be restored (in real terms) to at least its pre-1975 level

Regional policy is simply too valuable to the nation to be kept on a parsimonious budget. No-one would deny that eliminating waste and inefficiency is a desirable goal; but eliminating waste should not be used as an excuse for eliminating regional policy. On the contrary, a considerable expansion of regional policy spending is called for if sustained **national growth** is to continue, and if the challenge of the **single European market** is to be met. The other EC countries know this and have responded accordingly. So too must Britain. There is no shortage of vital projects deserving of more government aid. In particular:

1. More resources should be aimed at stimulating the inward movement of manufacturing investment into the Assisted Areas
Britain is already attracting many Japanese and US firms seeking to set up production plants within the rapidly integrating EC. The time is ripe for a revival of the much-maligned policy of using more regional aid to attract mobile *manufacturing* projects. And why just overseas firms? Not for many years has the overcrowded and high-labour-cost South East been in such a good position to act as a reservoir of firms which could be induced to move north.

2. More financial assistance should be offered to new firms, small firms and innovating firms in Assisted Areas
The 1988 reforms to regional policy were nowhere near sufficient to overcome the inherently poor economic environment facing small firms in depressed areas.

3. More resources should be devoted to improving the socio-economic infrastructure *of the Assisted Areas*
This involves more expenditure on social overhead capital (e.g. high-speed rail and road links to the Channel Tunnel), coupled with better **training programmes** for the long-term unemployed. These measures would help to solve a particularly difficult problem in the Assisted

Areas – the existence of large numbers of long-term unemployed persons.

Proposal 2: The geographical impact of all government fiscal policies should be monitored so that the regional impact of the government's own activities can be clearly seen and quickly changed

Incredibly, the UK has no system for regularly measuring the *regional* distribution of government spending. This should be rectified immediately. The persistent centralization of the civil service in London at a time of major recruitment difficulties and high wages in the capital defies economic logic. The **civil service dispersal programme** begun in the 1970s (following the Hardman Report of 1974) should be dramatically increased. Recent dispersal plans are far from adequate.

This should, however, be only the start. Every government spending programme needs to be examined and converted, where feasible, into a potential regional policy instrument. Why, for example, does the south get well over its fair share of **defence spending** each year? Why do nationalized industries have their headquarters and the best-paid executive jobs in London? Why are government research contracts concentrated in research institutions in the South East? These, and many other hard questions, must be continuously asked.

Proposal 3: All regional development initiatives should be coordinated

The delivery system of regional policy is in a mess. Hundreds of organizations, from the EC down to local councils and local self-help Enterprise Agencies, are now involved in regional policy. Many have no idea what other organizations involved in regional economic development in their own region are up to. There is no clear division of responsibility and there is consequently a great **overlapping of functions** and activities.

Moreover, there is no consistency from area to area. For example, Scotland and Wales are allowed development agencies while English regions are not. Large cities are allowed only borough councils while other areas have both district and county councils (both of which can run economic development initiatives).

Chaos is a recipe for the misuse of funds. Action is urgently required:

- to clarify the powers of those involved, especially the role of local councils and regional development agencies;

- to establish a system for the **coordination of policy initiatives** for regional economic development – Britain is almost unique in not having a system of regional economic planning.

Proposal 4: Regional development agencies should be created for all regions

Four reasons can be advanced in support of the proposal for **regional development agencies**. Firstly, the existing agencies in Scotland and Wales are almost universally regarded as having been highly successful. They have been so successful, in fact, that they have been suggested as possible targets for privatization. They have proved their worth under the most adverse economic circumstances.

Secondly, the agencies offer an excellent opportunity for improving regional policy coordination by drawing local councils, private businesses and local self-help institutions (e.g. Local Enterprise Agencies) together into a common programme.

Thirdly, regional agencies are better placed to draw on **local knowledge and expertise** so essential for the success of the newer types of regional policy now in operation (e.g. policies directed towards small firms, service industries and innovations). The EC and UK governments are too remote from the regions to administer these new policies efficiently.

Finally, regional agencies offer an excellent mechanism for overcoming the fears and prejudices of financial institutions based in London. They offer an excellent conduit along which private sector funds can flow to the depressed areas.

Our own preference would be for regional development agencies to be established in *all* regions, including the South East. The South East, after all, has some serious problems of its own – it has depressed inner-city areas and a severe problem of dilapidated and heavily over-used public infrastructure. These are suitable targets for the work of a development agency. Of course, the government would have to ensure that the northern agencies were more generously funded than those in the south. Otherwise the southern agencies would simply out-compete those in the north and cause regional disparities to widen even further.

Conclusion

The 1990s will usher in a new era for regional policy in Britain. Gone are the days when Whitehall had sole control over regional policy and when large manufacturing plants were seen as the best solution to regional problems. In the 1990s, regional policy will be a cooperative venture involving the EC, the central government and a host of development organizations 'on the ground' in the depressed areas.

The role of the EC in particular is likely to grow quickly in the 1990s. The future for the regional development agencies and local councils is less clear. If they are restricted (e.g. if agencies are privatized and if council involvement in economic development is curtailed), then new types of organization will have to be created at the local level. This is because the newer types of regional policy require strong local involvement. Selective assistance, help for small firms and innovation policies all require a substantial input of local knowledge and expertise.

When an in-depth history of regional policy in the 1980s is written, perhaps what will be highlighted most is the *survival* of regional policy. In an era of governments strongly committed to free enterprise, and with high unemployment in all regions, its survival was far from guaranteed. The fact that it *has* survived is testimony to the value of regional policy to the whole nation – to prosperous and depressed areas alike. The creation of the single European market in 1992 will confer an even greater importance on regional policy than before. It is essential that regional policy rises to the challenges it will face in the 1990s.

KEY WORDS

Real regional policy
    expenditure
Nationwide recession
Regional Development
    Grant
SMEs
Macroeconomic factors
Stop-go
National growth
Single European market
Infrastructure

Training programmes
Civil service dispersal
    programme
Defence spending
Overlapping of functions
Coordination of policy
    initiatives
Regional development
    agencies
Local knowledge and
    expertise

Index